Life-Changing Lessons I Learned Too Late: Wisdom, I Wish I Had Known At My First Job

Fast Forward Your Career: Insights to Accelerate Your Professional Journey

Ignatious Antony

Dedication

To my family, whose unwavering support and encouragement have guided me every step of the way.

To my parents, whose love and sacrifices have been my constant source of strength and inspiration.

To my friends, whose belief in me has never wavered, even in the face of challenges.

To my mentors and teachers, who have inspired me to reach for the stars and believe in the power of perseverance and hard work.

To the dreamers and the doers, who remind us that everything is possible with a journey of clear purpose, resilience, perseverance and actions.

And to all who strive to create their own good future, may this book serve as a guide and a testament to the power within you.

With deepest appreciation and gratitude,

Ignatious Antony

Acknowledgements

I am deeply grateful to many people who have supported and inspired me throughout the journey of writing this book.

First and foremost, my heartfelt thanks go to my beloved wife, Annie. Your unwavering love, patience, and encouragement have been my greatest sources of strength. To my son, Anil, and my daughter, Aneena, thank you for your understanding and always being a source of joy and inspiration.

I wish to pay special tribute to my late father and mother, Antony and Celine, whose wisdom and guidance continue to influence my life. Thank you for your endless love and support.

I am grateful to my elder sister, Ms. Baby Varghese, for her constant support and encouragement. My brothers, Dr. Paul Chakkalakkal and James C.A., have helped me immensely in my journey so far. I am profoundly grateful to them.

Finally, I sincerely thank all my teachers who taught me to read and write. Your dedication and passion for teaching have shaped who I am today, and I am eternally grateful.

Ignatious Antony

Published by: Ignatious Antony

First Edition: June 2024

Disclaimer:

This book is intended for informational purposes only. The views expressed in this book are the author's own and do not constitute professional advice. The author and publisher disclaim any liability for any direct, indirect, incidental, or consequential damages arising from using the information provided in this book. The reader is encouraged to seek professional guidance and conduct their own research before making any decisions based on the information contained herein.

Contact Us:

Please send all your suggestions and remarks in the following.

 email id: ignatious.luck@gmail.com

Table of Contents

Introduction

You are about to embark on a journey that will set the foundation for a successful and fulfilling career. This book is your guide, with practical advice and inspiring examples to help you build a strong professional foundation. Just like building a house, your career requires a solid foundation. Imagine laying the groundwork for a successful career by excelling in your first job assignment. By setting the right tone and establishing a solid foundation, you'll be well on your way to achieving your career goals.

As you progress through your career, actively seeking out opportunities for growth and learning is essential. Imagine a tree that continues to grow taller and stronger by reaching towards the sun. Similarly, embrace professional growth opportunities to expand your skills and expertise. This will enhance your professional capabilities and open doors to new experiences and challenges.

Building strong professional **relationships** is another crucial aspect of career success. Imagine a spider weaving an intricate web to catch its prey. To support your career advancement, build a network of strong professional relationships. These connections will provide valuable insights, mentorship, and opportunities for collaboration.

Mastering the art of time management is also vital for balancing work responsibilities and personal life. Imagine juggling multiple balls in the air with precision and ease. With strong time management skills, you can seamlessly navigate your work tasks and personal commitments. This will allow you to stay organised, focused, and productive, ensuring you achieve your goals and maintain a healthy work-life balance.

Throughout this book, you'll find inspiring stories, practical tips, and actionable advice to help you build a strong foundation for your career. By the end of this journey, this book will equip you with the tools and strategies needed to thrive in any work environment and achieve long-term success.

So, what are you waiting for? Let's start and lay the foundation for a successful and fulfilling career. As you embark on this journey, remember that every step you take is a building block towards your future success. Embrace the challenges, celebrate the victories, and keep pushing forward. Your career is a marathon, not a sprint, and with the proper foundation, growth mindset, relationships, and time management skills, you're well on your way to achieving greatness. Let's get started!

Excelling in Your First Job: Key Strategies for Success

Jumping into your first professional role is an exciting challenge that requires adaptability, relationship-building, and time management. Transitioning from school or past jobs into the professional world means getting a solid grasp of workplace culture, a crucial element for your overall success. This guide is here to give you the essential strategies to help you confidently and purposefully navigate the start of your career.

Embracing Workplace Culture

The key to rocking your first job is adapting to your organisation's unique culture. This means understanding its core values, principles, and unspoken norms and practices. Every workplace has its own vibe, and figuring out these nuances will make a huge difference in how well you fit in.

For example, if your company values collaboration and innovation, dive into brainstorming sessions and offer creative solutions. As legendary management consultant Peter Drucker said, "Culture eats strategy for breakfast." Embracing and understanding your workplace's cultural fabric can have a massive impact on your professional journey.

Building Professional Relationships

Building strong professional relationships is essential for success. Key components include networking, seeking mentorship, and mastering effective communication. Networking isn't just about growing your contact list; it's about creating meaningful connections that can support your professional growth.

Find mentors who can share guidance and wisdom from their experiences. Open and honest communication with colleagues and supervisors will build trust and encourage collaboration. Remember the wise words of American author John C. Maxwell: ***"People don't care how much you know until they know how much you care."***

Mastering Time Management

Effective time management is a linchpin for productivity and stress reduction. Prioritise tasks, set achievable deadlines, and use productivity tools to keep track of your responsibilities. The Eisenhower Matrix, which categorises tasks into urgent, meaningful, and other categories, can be an invaluable tool in this regard.

Consider the approach of former Apple CEO Steve Jobs, known for his intense focus on essential tasks and delegating or discarding the non-essential. Implementing such strategies will help you stay organised and maximise your time at work.

Setting and Achieving Career Goals

Setting clear, actionable career goals is essential for growth and advancement in your chosen field. Begin with short-term objectives that align with your long-term aspirations. Regularly review and adjust these goals to ensure they remain relevant and attainable.

Setting and achieving career goals can be likened to climbing a mountain. No matter how small, each step brings you closer to the summit. As motivational speaker Zig Ziglar aptly said***, "What you get by achieving your goals is not as important as what you become by achieving your goals."***

Thriving in your first job requires a multifaceted approach encompassing cultural adaptation, relationship-building, time management, and goal-setting. By embracing these strategies, you can confidently and purposefully navigate the early days of your career, laying a solid foundation for future success.

Adapting to Workplace Culture

Starting your professional journey involves more than just mastering your job responsibilities; it requires a deep understanding of your company's values, norms, and expectations. Aligning your behaviour with these core beliefs and principles is crucial for smoothly integrating into your new environment and excelling in your role.

Recognising Core Beliefs and Principles

The first step in adapting to workplace culture is identifying the company's core beliefs and principles. Every organisation operates on values that guide its actions and decisions. The company's mission statement or code of conduct often enshrines these values. For example, if innovation is a cornerstone of your company, displaying creativity and a willingness to take risks in your daily tasks is very important. Embracing these values fosters a sense of belonging and enhances your contributions to the organisation's mission.

Reflecting on the words of business magnate Richard Branson, ***"Clients do not come first. Employees come first. They will care for the clients if you care for your employees."*** This underscores the importance of internalising company values for overall success.

Unwritten Rules and Practices

Beyond the explicitly stated values, every workplace has a set of unwritten rules and practices that can be more influential than official policies. For instance, while formal communication channels are outlined in the company book, most people prefer using informal tools like Slack or group chats for quick updates. Observing and adapting to these practices will help you integrate more effectively. Asking colleagues about these unwritten norms during your initial days can be incredibly beneficial, demonstrating your eagerness to learn and adapt and earning you immediate respect.

Building Rapport with Team Members

Building solid relationships with your team members is essential for your professional success. When you demonstrate an understanding and respect for your company's culture, it becomes easier for others to connect with you. If teamwork and collaboration are highly valued, actively participating in team meetings and offering your assistance on projects can endear you to your colleagues. Establishing these connections early in your career provides a solid support network and smoother your transition.

The well-known proverb, ***"No man is an island,"*** emphasizes the importance of fostering a supportive community within your workplace.

Demonstrating Professionalism

Respecting established workplace norms is crucial. Demonstrating professionalism by adhering to these norms showcases your adaptability and respect for the organisational culture. If punctuality is a critical value in your workplace, arriving on Time for meetings and deadlines reflects positively on you. Similarly, if the workplace has a casual dress code but you have an essential meeting, dressing appropriately shows that you are mindful of the context and can adapt accordingly.

Simple gestures, like greeting everyone in the morning, joining office events, and acknowledging your coworkers' efforts, can significantly contribute to building a positive team spirit. These actions reflect your commitment to being a part of the team and respecting the organisational culture. Over Time, these small efforts accumulate into a reputation for being professional and adaptable.

Fostering a Sense of Belonging

Implementing company values in your daily tasks fosters a sense of belonging within the organisation. Consistently aligning your actions with the company's core principles makes you an integral part of the organisation. For instance, if customer satisfaction is crucial, addressing client concerns can set you apart as a dedicated employee. Your commitment to upholding these values in every aspect of your job will not go unnoticed and can lead to better career opportunities within the organisation.

When you embody the company's ethos, you strengthen your position within the team. For example, if sustainability is a core value, initiating or supporting eco-friendly projects shows your dedication to the company's long-term goals. This degree of involvement shows that you are committed to the company's success, not just interested in earning a paycheck.

Adapting to Cultural Evolution

Company culture is not static; it evolves. Adapting to these changes is critical for long-term success. Research suggests that cultural fit is less about static alignment and more about how quickly employees can adapt as the organisational culture changes. Staying flexible and open to change ensures you remain relevant and valuable to the organisation.

For instance, the rise of remote and hybrid work models during the COVID-19 pandemic significantly impacted company cultures. Organisations that adapted their approach and maintained a strong culture saw better employee engagement and retention rates. As a new employee, embracing these changes and contributing to the evolving culture can enhance your standing within the company.

Leveraging Professional Development

Active participation in the company's professional development opportunities can further solidify your understanding of its values and norms. Many organisations offer training sessions, workshops, and seminars aimed at helping employees grow within the company's cultural framework. Attending these sessions broadens your skill set and demonstrates your commitment to the organisation's ethos.

Seeking Feedback and Mentorship

Seeking feedback from your supervisors and peers is beneficial during your integration period. Constructive criticism can offer insights into areas where you might need to adjust your behaviour or approach. Regularly asking for feedback shows dedication to continuous improvement and seriousness about fitting into the company culture.

Building relationships with mentors provides valuable guidance on navigating the company's cultural landscape. Experienced professionals can offer advice on handling specific situations, understanding unwritten rules, and aligning more closely with the company's values. Establishing these mentor-mentee relationships early on can accelerate your learning curve and help you make a positive impact quickly.

Conclusion

Adapting to workplace culture involves:

- Recognising core beliefs.

- Understanding unwritten norms.

- Building professional relationships.

- Demonstrating professionalism.

- Fostering a sense of belonging.

- Adapting to cultural evolution.

- Leveraging professional development.

- Seeking feedback and mentorship.

By embracing these strategies, you can confidently and purposefully navigate your new professional environment, paving the way for a successful and fulfilling career.

Time Management Skills

Enhancing productivity through effective time management techniques is crucial for success in your first job. This section will delve into essential time management skills that can help you maximise your efficiency and reduce stress. By prioritising tasks, overcoming procrastination, breaking down more significant projects, and setting deadlines, you can manage your Time more effectively and achieve your career goals.

Prioritising Tasks

Prioritising tasks based on urgency and importance is fundamental. The Eisenhower Matrix is a powerful tool that can help you categorise tasks to optimise time usage. This technique divides tasks into four quadrants: urgent and important, important but not urgent, urgent but not necessary, and neither urgent nor essential. Focusing on urgent and vital tasks ensures that critical deadlines are met and prevents last-minute rushes. Important but not urgent tasks can be scheduled for later, while urgent but unimportant tasks can be delegated or minimised. Items that fall into the last category should be avoided or tackled only when they become more pressing.

Overcoming Procrastination

Recognising common triggers of procrastination is vital to effective time management. Procrastination can significantly hinder productivity, leading to increased stress and missed deadlines. Understanding why you procrastinate can help you implement strategies to overcome it. Common triggers include feeling overwhelmed by large tasks, lack of clear deadlines, fear of failure, and distractions from social media or other sources. Try breaking tasks into smaller, more manageable steps to combat these triggers. This can make daunting projects feel less intimidating and provide a clear roadmap for completion.

Setting Specific Deadlines

Setting specific deadlines is another effective strategy to promote task completion and time management. Setting firm deadlines for yourself makes you more likely to stay focused and avoid procrastination. It's also beneficial to share your deadlines with colleagues or supervisors, creating a sense of accountability. Knowing that others know your timelines can motivate you to stay on track.

Implementing Accountability Measures

Accountability measures can significantly enhance productivity. Accountability can come in many forms, such as regular check-ins with a mentor or manager, using a project management tool to track progress, or working with a colleague who holds you accountable for meeting your deadlines. Creating an accountability system helps you stay focused and committed to your goals.

Limiting Distractions

Distractions like email notifications, social media, and unnecessary meetings can derail your workflow.

Implementing strategies to minimise these distractions can help you stay on task. For example, schedule specific times to check email and turn off notifications outside of those times. Use productivity tools or browser extensions that block distracting websites during work hours. Setting boundaries with colleagues and communicating your need for uninterrupted work time can further reduce distractions.

Batching Similar Tasks

Another effective technique is batching similar tasks together. By grouping tasks that require similar resources or brainpower, you can complete them more efficiently. For instance, if you have several reports to write, tackling them all at once can save Time compared to switching between writing and other unrelated tasks. This technique reduces the mental energy required to switch gears and helps maintain a steady workflow.

Taking Regular Breaks

It's essential to leave room for breaks in your schedule. Taking short, regular breaks can improve overall productivity and well-being. Micro-breaks of ten minutes or less help reduce fatigue and maintain focus throughout the day. Use this Time to stretch, take a walk, or relax your mind before diving back into work.

Understanding the Pareto Principle

The Pareto Principle, or the 80/20 rule, can help you work smarter. This principle states that 80% of your results come from 20% of your efforts. Identifying and focusing on the most impactful tasks can lead to greater productivity. Evaluate your to-do list regularly and concentrate on activities that drive the most significant outcomes. By amplifying these high-impact tasks, you can maximise your effectiveness and achieve your goals more efficiently.

Embracing Goal Setting

Setting clear and achievable goals gives you direction and motivation. The SMART model—specific, Measurable, Achievable, Relevant, and Time-bound—can help you establish both short-term and long-term objectives. Short-term goals might include completing a weekly report, while long-term goals could involve earning a promotion within a year. Breaking down these goals into actionable steps makes tracking progress and staying motivated easier.

Creating a Detailed Time Management Plan

Mapping out your daily, weekly, and monthly schedules allows you to allocate Time effectively. Start by identifying upcoming deadlines, then work backward to estimate how much Time each task will require. Block off specific times on your calendar for focused work and ensure you incorporate regular breaks. Using digital tools like Google Calendar can help you stay organised and provide a visual representation of your commitments.

Balancing Work and Personal Life

Maintaining a balance between work and personal life is vital for sustainable productivity. Overworking can lead to burnout, so setting boundaries and reserving Time for self-care is essential. Ensure you sleep well, exercise regularly, eat balanced meals, and socialise with friends and family. Taking care of your physical and mental well-being can enhance your focus and energy levels at work, ultimately boosting your productivity.

Conclusion

Effective time management is crucial for enhancing productivity and reducing stress in your first job. Here are key strategies to help you manage your time more effectively and achieve your career goals:

- Prioritise tasks
- Overcome procrastination
- Set specific deadlines
- Implement accountability measures
- Limit distractions
- Batch similar tasks
- Take regular breaks
- Understand the Pareto Principle
- Embrace goal setting
- Create a detailed time management plan
- Balance work and personal life

Adopting these practices allows you to manage your time more effectively and achieve your career goals.

Unleash Your Potential with a Compelling Vision!

Imagine having a clear, inspiring vision for your life—a compelling vision that pulls you forward, motivating you to take action daily. You can achieve anything if you have empowering beliefs about your potential and sub-goals to keep you on track. It's never too late to create the life of your dreams. Let's explore how you can unleash your potential by crafting a powerful vision.

Envision Your Ideal Future: Visualise Your Dreams in Vivid Detail

Start by envisioning your ideal future. What does it look, sound, and feel like? Take a moment to immerse yourself in this vision. Picture yourself achieving your goals, living your dreams, and experiencing joy and fulfilment. The more specific you get, the more powerful your vision will become.

Spend 10-15 minutes each day visualising your ideal future. Close your eyes, take deep breaths, and paint a detailed mental picture of your dream life.

"The only limit to our realisation of tomorrow is our doubts of today." — Franklin D. Roosevelt.

Set Clear, Specific Goals

What do you want to achieve? Whether starting a business, writing a book, or travelling the world, define your goals clearly. Specificity is key. Instead of saying, "I want to travel," specify, "I want to visit Japan and explore its culture for two weeks."

Write down your top three goals in precise detail. Place this list somewhere you can see it daily to remind yourself of your aspirations.

Example: Instead of a vague goal like "get fit," set a specific goal such as "run a 5K marathon in six months."

Break Down Your Big Dreams

Create Sub-Goals

Big dreams can seem overwhelming. To make them more manageable, break them down into smaller, actionable steps. Each sub-goal should be a stepping stone towards your larger vision.

List the sub-goals needed to achieve each of your main goals and create a timeline for them to stay on track.

"The journey of a thousand miles begins with one step." — Lao Tzu

Celebrate Small Wins

Every step forward is a victory. Celebrate your small wins to stay motivated and keep momentum. Recognising progress, no matter how small, fuels your drive to keep going.

Keep a journal to track your achievements. Reflect on your progress weekly and celebrate your milestones.

Example: If you want to write a book, celebrate completing each chapter or reaching a certain word count.

Examine and Empower Your Beliefs

Identify Limiting Beliefs

Your beliefs can either propel you forward or hold you back. Identify any limiting thoughts that might be sabotaging your progress. Replace "I'm not good enough" with "I'm capable of anything I set my mind to."

Write down any negative beliefs you have about yourself. Next to each one, write a positive affirmation that counters it.

"Whether you think you can, or you think you can't—you're right." — Henry Ford

Use Affirmations to Shift Your Mindset

Affirmations are powerful tools for shifting mindsets. Repeating positive statements helps rewire your brain to believe in your capabilities.

Create a list of affirmations that resonate with your goals and vision. Repeat them daily, preferably in front of a mirror.

Example: If you doubt your abilities, say, "I am confident and capable of achieving my goals" every morning.

Surround Yourself with Supportive People

Build a Positive Network

Surround yourself with people who believe in you and your vision. Their encouragement and support can make a significant difference in your journey. Seek out mentors, join communities, and build a network of positive influences.

Identify individuals who inspire you and reach out to them. Attend events or join groups where you can meet like-minded people.

"Surround yourself with only people who are going to lift you higher." — Oprah Winfrey

Share Your Vision

Sharing your vision with others makes it more real and holds you accountable. When you articulate your dreams, you inspire yourself and attract support and opportunities.

Discuss your goals and vision with friends, family, or colleagues. Share updates on your progress and seek feedback.

If you want to start a business, share your business plan with a mentor or business group for advice and encouragement.

Implementing These Principles

Daily Visualisation

Make visualisation a daily habit. It reinforces your goals and keeps your vision vivid in your mind. The more you visualise, the more motivated you'll be to take action.

Set aside time each day for visualisation. Create a quiet space, close your eyes, and vividly imagine achieving your goals.

Consistent Goal Setting and Reviewing

Review and adjust your goals and sub-goals regularly. Consistent goal setting helps you stay on track and adapt to changes or new insights.

Review your goals weekly. Adjust your sub-goals as needed and set new ones based on your progress.

Example: If you're making faster progress than expected, set more ambitious sub-goals to keep challenging yourself.

Affirmations and Positive Self-Talk

Incorporate affirmations into your daily routine. Positive self-talk boosts your confidence and keeps you focused on your strengths and potential.

A Repeat your affirmations in the morning and before bed. Carry a list of them with you for quick reference during the day.

Engage with Your Support Network

Stay actively engaged with your support network. Share your progress, celebrate your wins, and seek advice when needed. Positive reinforcement from others keeps you motivated and accountable.

Schedule regular check-ins with your mentors or support group. Update them on your progress and seek their insights.

Conclusion

Unleashing your potential with a compelling vision involves clarity, belief, and action. You can achieve anything by envisioning your ideal future, setting specific goals, breaking them down into manageable steps, empowering your beliefs, and surrounding yourself with supportive people. Imagine the life you could lead with this powerful combination: the relationships you'd build, the experiences you'd have, the impact you'd make. It's always possible to start living your best life. Your vision is waiting — are you ready to make it a reality?

Setting and Achieving Career Goals

To excel and find fulfilment in your first job, it is crucial to identify both short-term and long-term career goals and create actionable plans to achieve them. Clear objectives provide direction and motivation and provide a roadmap for professional growth. Here are some critical strategies for setting and attaining career goals:

Defining Clear and Specific Goals

Defining clear and specific career goals is essential. Without particular targets, it's easy to drift aimlessly in your professional life. Think about what you want to achieve in the next six months, year, or five years. These goals could range from gaining new skills, receiving promotions, or transitioning into different roles within your field. According to the Psychological Bulletin, writing down and monitoring your goals increases the chances of achieving them by making the outcomes more concrete and trackable. Clear goals provide clarity and focus, helping you stay on course even when challenges arise.

Developing Actionable Steps and Milestones

Once you have defined your goals, develop actionable steps and milestones that lead towards them. This process involves breaking down larger objectives into smaller, manageable tasks. For example, if your long-term goal is to become a project manager, identify the skills and experiences required for that role. This might include taking specific courses, seeking relevant projects, or volunteering for leadership positions. Segmenting your goals into achievable milestones allows you to make consistent progress without feeling overwhelmed. The SMART criteria—Specific, Measurable, Attainable, Relevant, and Time-bound—are an excellent structure for this purpose. Specific goals offer clarity; measurable goals enable progress tracking; achievable goals sustain motivation; relevant goals ensure alignment with broader aspirations; and time-bound goals establish deadlines for increased accountability.

Seeking Feedback and Guidance

Seeking feedback and guidance from mentors and supervisors is another crucial step in refining your goal-setting strategies. Mentors can provide invaluable insights and advice based on their experiences, which can be particularly helpful in identifying realistic and impactful goals. Regular discussions with mentors and supervisors help ensure your goals remain relevant to industry trends and company expectations. Feedback-driven goals incorporating regular constructive feedback play a significant role in professional development, keeping you aligned with evolving circumstances. Not only does this approach improve your performance, but it also shows your willingness to grow and adapt, qualities highly valued in any professional setting.

Celebrating Achievements and Learning from Setbacks

Celebrating achievements and learning from setbacks are integral parts of the goal-setting process. Acknowledging your successes, no matter how small, boosts confidence and reinforces the behaviours that contribute to achieving your objectives. Celebrations do not need to be grand; even simple acknowledgements like sharing your accomplishments with friends or treating yourself to something special can be incredibly motivating. On the other hand, setbacks should be viewed as learning opportunities rather than failures. Analyse what went wrong, understand why it happened, and adjust your plans accordingly. This practice fosters resilience and perseverance, ensuring continuous improvement and progress toward your career aspirations. Engaging in this reflective practice consistently contributes to both personal and professional growth.

Setting Stretch Goals

In addition to these steps, setting stretch goals can propel you beyond your comfort zone, encouraging innovation and personal growth. While these goals may not always meet the 'achievable' criterion of the SMART framework, they stimulate creativity and ambition. For instance, if you aim to double your sales numbers within six months, you might not hit the target, but your efforts and strategies will likely result in significant improvement. Stretch goals challenge you to think outside the box and explore new methods, ultimately leading to breakthroughs in your professional development.

Utilising SWOT Analysis

SWOT analysis is another effective method to inform your goal-setting process. By analysing your strengths, weaknesses, opportunities, and threats, you comprehensively understand your current position and what you need to improve or leverage. This holistic approach allows you to set more informed and strategic goals. For example, recognising a personal strength such as strong analytical skills can lead you to seek roles or projects where these skills are advantageous while identifying a weakness like lack of public speaking experience, which might prompt you to take a communication course or join a speaking club.

Aligning Personal Aspirations with Professional Goals

Aligning personal aspirations with professional goals enhances commitment and determination. Understanding what truly motivates you personally—and integrating these motivations into your professional goals—creates a sense of purpose and satisfaction. Whether it's financial stability, creative expression, or a desire to make a difference, knowing your "why" helps maintain focus and drive.

Periodically Reviewing and Adjusting Goals

Reviewing and adjusting your goals is vital for fostering continuous growth and progress. The dynamic nature of the workplace means that goals may need to evolve to stay relevant. Regularly assess your objectives, celebrate milestones, and adjust based on new insights and external changes. This ensures you remain adaptable and responsive to new opportunities and challenges.

Conclusion

Setting and achieving career goals involves:

- Defining clear objectives.
- Developing actionable steps.
- Seeking feedback.
- Celebrating achievements.
- Setting stretch goals.
- Utilising SWOT analysis.
- Aligning personal aspirations with professional goals.
- Periodically reviewing and adjusting your plans.

By implementing these strategies, you can navigate your career path with confidence and purpose, ensuring long-term success and fulfilment.

Building Strong Relationships: The Key to Unlocking Opportunities

In the professional world, building strong relationships is more than just a nice-to-have; it's a crucial element for success. Networking and maintaining meaningful relationships can open doors to countless opportunities and support systems. As American author and motivational speaker Zig Ziglar once said, "You can have everything in life you want if you will just help other people get what they want." This statement encapsulates the essence of networking and relationship-building.

The Importance of Strong Relationships

Strong professional relationships offer numerous benefits:

1. **Opportunities for Advancement**: Networking can lead to job offers, promotions, and career advancements. Many job opportunities are never advertised and are filled through referrals and recommendations from trusted connections.

2. **Support Systems**: Professional relationships provide emotional and practical support during challenging times. Colleagues, mentors, and peers can offer advice, share their experiences, and provide encouragement.

3. **Knowledge Sharing**: Networking allows for the exchange of ideas, knowledge, and expertise.

Learning from others' experiences can provide new perspectives and solutions to problems.

4. **Increased Visibility**: Being well-connected can increase your visibility in your industry, making you more likely to be considered for opportunities.

5. **Strategies to Build Strong Relationships**

6. **Be Genuine and Authentic**: Authenticity is the foundation of any strong relationship. Show genuine interest in others, listen actively, and be yourself. As Oscar Wilde said, "Be yourself; everyone else is already taken."

7. **Attend Networking Events**: Participate in industry conferences, seminars, and social gatherings. These events provide excellent opportunities to meet new people and expand your professional network.

8. **Leverage Social Media**: Platforms like LinkedIn are invaluable for networking. Connect with industry professionals, join relevant groups, and engage with content to build an online presence.

9. **Seek Mentorship**: Find a mentor who can provide guidance, feedback, and support. Mentors can help you navigate your career path and introduce you to their network.

10. **Offer Help and Value**: Networking is a two-way street. Offer your assistance, share your knowledge, and add value to others. Helping others can

strengthen your relationships and create a positive reputation.

11. **Follow-Up**: After meeting someone new, follow up with a personalised message. Keep in touch with your connections regularly to maintain and strengthen your relationships.

12. **Join Professional Organisations**: Join industry-specific organisations or groups. These communities provide opportunities for networking, professional development, and collaboration.

13. **Attend Workshops and Training**: Engage in continuous learning by attending workshops and training sessions. These settings enhance your skills and provide opportunities to meet like-minded professionals.

14. **Be Respectful and Considerate**: Respect others' time, opinions, and boundaries. Being considerate and respectful builds trust and credibility.

15. **Cultivate Emotional Intelligence**: Develop empathy, active listening, and self-awareness skills. Emotional intelligence enhances your ability to connect with others on a deeper level.

Conclusion

Building strong professional relationships is essential for unlocking opportunities and creating a robust support system. You can cultivate meaningful relationships that will benefit your career by being genuine, offering value, and actively participating in networking activities. As John C. Maxwell aptly stated, **"People may hear your words, but they feel your attitude."** Approach relationship-building with a positive attitude and genuine intent, and you will see wide doors of opportunity open.

Financial Literacy is Crucial: A Path to Greater Financial Stability

Financial literacy is an essential skill that profoundly impacts personal and professional life. Understanding how to manage money, invest, and save early on can lead to greater financial stability and freedom. As financial expert Robert Kiyosaki famously said, ***"It's not how much money you make, but how much money you keep, how hard it works for you, and how many generations you keep it for."*** This statement underscores the importance of financial literacy in achieving long-term success and stability.

The Importance of Financial Literacy

1. **Enhanced Financial Stability**: Financial literacy helps one make informed decisions about spending, saving, and investing, which leads to financial stability.

2. **Reduced Stress and Anxiety**: Understanding and managing finances effectively can significantly reduce the stress and anxiety associated with financial uncertainties.

3. **Improved Decision-Making**: Knowledge of financial principles allows for better decision-making, from everyday purchases to major investments.

4. **Long-Term Security**: Proper financial planning and investing can ensure long-term security and prepare for future needs and emergencies.

5. **Empowerment and Independence**: Financial literacy empowers individuals to take control of their financial

future, leading to greater independence and confidence.

Strategies to Achieve Financial Literacy

1. **Educate Yourself**: Start by educating yourself about basic financial concepts such as budgeting, saving, investing, and debt management. Numerous books, online courses, and resources are available for learning.

    a. George S. Clason's "The Richest Man in Babylon" is an excellent introduction to fundamental financial principles.
    b. Websites like Investopedia and Khan Academy offer comprehensive guides and courses on various financial topics.

2. **Create a Budget**: Establishing a budget is the cornerstone of financial management. Track your income and expenses to understand where your money is going and identify areas for saving.

    a. To maintain your budget effectively, use budgeting tools and apps like Mint, YNAB (You Need A Budget), or Excel spreadsheets.

3. **Save Regularly**: Develop a habit of regularly saving a portion of your income. Aim to save at least 20% of your income, but adjust based on your financial goals and obligations.

    a. Set up automatic transfers to a savings account to ensure consistency in saving.

4. **Invest Wisely**: Investing is crucial for growing your wealth. Understand different investment options such as stocks, bonds, mutual funds, and real estate.

    a. Consider starting with low-cost index funds or ETFs (Exchange-Traded Funds), which offer diversification and lower risk than individual stocks.

5. **Manage Debt**: Learn to manage and reduce debt effectively. Prioritise paying off high-interest debt first and avoid accumulating unnecessary debt.

    a. Use strategies like the debt snowball or debt avalanche methods to pay off debts systematically.

6. **Plan for Retirement**: Start planning for retirement early by contributing to retirement accounts such as 401(k)s, IRAs, or other pension plans.

    a. Take advantage of employer-matched contributions and maximise your contributions to benefit from compound interest.

7. **Build an Emergency Fund**: To cover unexpected expenses or financial emergencies, establish an emergency fund. Aim to save at least three to six months' worth of living expenses.

    a. Keep the emergency fund in a high-yield savings account for easy access and growth.

8. **Seek Professional Advice**: If needed, seek advice from financial advisors or planners to help you create a comprehensive financial plan tailored to your goals.

    a. Ensure the advisor is certified (e.g., CFP - Certified Financial Planner) and has a fiduciary duty to act in your best interest.

9. **Stay Informed**: Stay updated with the latest financial news and trends. Understanding the economic environment can help you make informed financial decisions.

    a. Subscribe to financial news sources such as Bloomberg, CNBC, or financial sections of major newspapers.

10. **Practise Financial Discipline**: Cultivate habits of financial discipline, such as avoiding impulsive purchases, living within your means, and regularly reviewing your financial plans.

    a. Establish financial goals and regularly monitor your progress towards achieving them.

Conclusion

Financial literacy is crucial for achieving financial stability and independence. Here are key strategies to help you take control of your financial future:

- Educate yourself
- Create a budget
- Save regularly
- Invest wisely
- Manage debt
- Plan for retirement
- Build an emergency fund
- Seek professional advice
- Stay Informed
- Practise financial discipline

As Warren Buffett wisely said, ***"Do not save what is left after spending; instead, spend what is left after saving."*** Implement these strategies to secure your financial well-being and enjoy a more prosperous and secure future.

Invest in Yourself: The Best Investment You Can Make

Investing in yourself is the most valuable investment you can make. Continuous self-improvement through education, hobbies, and self-care enhances your skills and knowledge and enriches your overall well-being and happiness. As the renowned investor Warren Buffett once said, "The best investment you can make is in yourself." This quote underscores the significance of dedicating time and resources to personal growth and development.

The Importance of Investing in Yourself

1. **Skill Enhancement**: Continuously learning and acquiring new skills keeps you competitive and adaptable in an ever-changing job market.
2. **Increased Confidence**: Self-improvement boosts your self-esteem and confidence, empowering you to take on new challenges.
3. **Better Health**: Investing in physical and mental health leads to a more fulfilling and productive life.
4. **Personal Fulfilment**: Pursuing hobbies and interests brings joy and satisfaction, enhancing the overall quality of life.
5. **Career Advancement**: Gaining new qualifications and expertise can open doors to better job opportunities and career progression.

Strategies to Invest in Yourself

1. **Continuous Education**: Never stop learning. Enrol in courses, attend workshops and pursue higher education to expand your knowledge and skills.
   a. Platforms like Coursera, Udemy, and LinkedIn Learning offer various online courses on various subjects.
   b. Consider formal education such as advanced degrees or certifications relevant to your career.
2. **Develop New Hobbies**: Hobbies stimulate creativity, reduce stress, and provide a sense of accomplishment.
   a. Explore activities like painting, gardening, playing a musical instrument, or learning a new language.
   b. Joining clubs or groups with similar interests can also help you connect with like-minded individuals.
3. **Prioritise Self-Care**: Taking care of your physical and mental health is crucial for overall well-being.
   a. Exercise regularly, eat a balanced diet and ensure you get enough sleep.
   b. Practise mindfulness and meditation to reduce stress and enhance mental clarity.
4. **Read Regularly**: Reading broadens your perspective and enhances your knowledge.
   a. Aim to read books on various topics, including personal development, fiction, and non-fiction.
   b. Join a book club to discuss and share insights with others.

5. **Set Personal Goals**: Define clear and achievable personal goals. Setting and achieving these goals provides a sense of direction and purpose.
   a. Set effective goals by using the SMART criteria (Specific, Measurable, Achievable, Relevant, and Time-bound).
6. **Seek Mentorship**: Find mentors who can provide guidance, share their experiences, and offer valuable advice.
   a. Mentorship can significantly accelerate your personal and professional growth.
7. **Network and Build Relationships**: Building a strong network of professional and personal relationships provides support, opportunities, and new perspectives.
   a. Attend networking events, join professional organisations, and maintain meaningful connections.
8. **Embrace Challenges**: Step out of your comfort zone and embrace new challenges. Overcoming challenges fosters resilience and personal growth.
   a. Take on new projects at work, volunteer for leadership roles, or try something entirely new.
9. **Reflect and Learn from Experiences**: Regularly reflect on and learn from your experiences. Self-reflection helps you understand your strengths and areas for improvement.
   a. Keep a journal to document your thoughts, achievements, and lessons learned.

10. **Manage Your Finances**: Financial stability is crucial to investing in yourself. Learn to manage your finances effectively to support your personal and professional growth.

    a. Create a budget, save regularly, and invest wisely.

Conclusion

Investing in yourself through continuous self-improvement, hobbies, and self-care pays dividends. Here are key ways to prioritise your personal growth and well-being:

- Prioritise education
- Develop new hobbies
- Take care of your health
- Read Regularly
- Set personal goals
- Seek mentorship
- Build relationships
- Embrace challenges
- Reflect on experiences
- Manage your finances

Focusing on these areas can enhance your skills, boost your confidence, and lead a more fulfilling and successful life. As Jim Rohn aptly said, ***"Work harder on yourself than you do on your job***." Investing in yourself creates a foundation for long-term success and personal satisfaction.

Embrace Failure as a Teacher: The Path to Personal Growth

Failure isn't the end; it's a valuable learning experience that can accelerate personal growth and development. Embracing failure early in life can lead to profound insights and significant progress. As Thomas Edison once said, *"I have not failed. I've just found 10,000 ways that won't work."* This quote highlights the importance of viewing failure not as a defeat but as a step toward eventual success.

The Importance of Embracing Failure

1. **Growth and Development**: Failure provides opportunities to learn and grow. Each setback teaches valuable lessons that contribute to personal and professional development.
2. **Resilience Building**: Overcoming failure strengthens resilience. Facing challenges and persevering builds a robust character capable of handling adversity.
3. **Innovation and Creativity**: Many great innovations result from learning from failures. Embracing failure encourages creative problem-solving and out-of-the-box thinking.
4. **Improved Decision-Making**: Learning from past mistakes leads to better decision-making. Understanding what went wrong helps in making more informed choices in the future.

5. **Self-Reflection**: Failure prompts self-reflection, allowing individuals to assess their actions, strategies, and goals. This introspection fosters personal growth and self-awareness.

Strategies to Embrace Failure

1. **Change Your Mindset**: Shift your perspective on failure. View it as a learning opportunity rather than a setback. Adopting a growth mindset helps you embrace challenges and learn from them.
   a. Carol Dweck's book "Mindset: The New Psychology of Success" explores the concept of a growth mindset and its benefits.
2. **Analyze and Learn**: After experiencing failure, analyse what went wrong. Identify the factors that led to the failure and the lessons that can be learned from it.
   a. Keeping a failure journal to document and reflect on setbacks can provide valuable insights and guide future actions.
3. **Seek Feedback**: Don't be afraid to seek feedback from others. Constructive criticism from mentors, peers, or supervisors can offer different perspectives and help identify areas for improvement.
   a. Regularly asking for feedback fosters a culture of continuous learning and growth.
4. **Stay Resilient**: Build resilience by developing coping strategies to deal with failure. Focus on maintaining a positive attitude, setting realistic goals, and taking proactive steps to overcome challenges.
   a.

b. Practices like mindfulness and meditation can enhance resilience and emotional stability.

5. **Celebrate Effort, Not Just Success**: Acknowledge and celebrate the effort put into a task, regardless of the outcome. Recognising hard work and dedication fosters a positive attitude towards failure.

   a. Create a culture that values learning and growth over perfection.

6. **Be Persistent**: Persistence is key to overcoming failure. Keep pushing forward, even when faced with setbacks. Every failure brings you one step closer to success.

   a. Thomas Edison's persistence in inventing the lightbulb is a classic example of how persistence leads to breakthrough success.

7. **Learn from Others**: Study the failures and successes of others. Understanding how successful people overcame their failures can provide inspiration.

   a. Reading biographies or listening to interviews of successful individuals can offer valuable lessons.

8. **Take Calculated Risks**: Don't be afraid to take risks. Calculated risks can lead to significant rewards. Embracing the possibility of failure is part of the journey to success.

   a. Evaluate the potential risks and rewards before making decisions to ensure they are well thought out.

9. **Develop Problem-Solving Skills**: Enhance your problem-solving abilities to navigate failures effectively.

Strong problem-solving skills enable you to find solutions and bounce back from setbacks.

   a. Engage in activities and training that challenge your problem-solving capabilities.

10. **Maintain a Support System**: Surround yourself with supportive people who encourage and uplift you during difficult times. A strong support system provides motivation and perspective.

   a. Build a network of friends, family, mentors, and colleagues who can offer support and guidance.

Conclusion

Embracing failure as a teacher is essential for personal growth and development. Here are key strategies to turn failures into valuable learning experiences:

- Change your mindset
- Analyze and learn from failures
- Seek feedback
- Stay resilient
- Celebrate effort
- Be persistent
- Learn from others
- Take calculated risks
- Develop problem-solving skills

As Henry Ford wisely said, ***"Failure is simply the opportunity to begin again, this time more intelligently."*** Embrace failure, learn from it, and let it propel you toward greater success and personal fulfilment.

Building Professional Relationships

Embarking on your first job is an exciting journey, and one of the keys to success lies in cultivating and nurturing valuable connections through networking, mentorship, and effective communication. These relationships can propel your career forward, provide essential support, and unlock new opportunities.

Expanding Your Professional Network

To kickstart your networking efforts, develop a plan to expand your professional circle. Begin by identifying events within and outside your company to meet potential mentors and peers. Attending seminars, industry conferences, and social gatherings can help you foster meaningful interactions. Go beyond your immediate circle and connect with individuals from diverse backgrounds, roles, and industries. This diversity will expose you to new perspectives and ideas that can be beneficial throughout your career.

Engaging in networking events can lead to numerous career advancement opportunities. Participating in these events allows you to showcase your skills and interests to others in your field. According to Zubair (2023), connecting with senior executives and industry professionals at these events can help define your career interests and build significant relationships. During these interactions, be proactive and approachable. Introduce yourself confidently and show genuine interest in others' work. Follow up with personalised messages to keep the connection alive.

Finding and Leveraging Mentorship

Once you've established initial contacts, seek guidance from experienced professionals. Finding a mentor can significantly accelerate your learning curve. A mentor could be a former peer, a career coach, or someone you meet at an event. Mentors offer career guidance and introduce you to their own networks. Leveraging your mentor's connections can enhance your professional development. Mentors can facilitate access to key individuals, providing opportunities you might have encountered with others.

Building relationships with your mentor and others in your network requires consistent effort. Nurture these relationships by regularly keeping in touch, asking for advice, and sharing your achievements and challenges. Be receptive to feedback and willing to implement suggestions. Effective communication is crucial here. Stay connected via email, instant messaging, and video conferencing. Choose the most appropriate mode for each situation—email for detailed information and video calls for complex discussions.

Engaging in Effective Communication

Engaging in mentorship is a two-way street. Be open to change and candid advice from your mentor. Applying the lessons learned from these interactions in real-world scenarios is vital. The practical knowledge gained will be invaluable as you navigate your career. Additionally, respecting boundaries in mentorship relationships is essential. Be mindful of your mentor's Time and availability, and avoid communication outside agreed-upon times.

Mentors can offer career guidance and support for long-term success. They can advise you on navigating workplace challenges, making strategic career moves, and developing necessary skills. Drawing from their experiences and insights can help you avoid common pitfalls. The relationship with your mentor should be built on trust, respect, and mutual benefit. As Holmes emphasises, clear expectations and active listening are fundamental to effective mentoring.

Networking in Everyday Interactions

Networking is not limited to formal events; everyday interactions at work also count. Take the initiative to introduce yourself to colleagues, join team projects, and participate in company activities. Being engaged and approachable demonstrates your willingness to be part of the team and can lead to informal mentoring relationships. These interactions are opportunities to learn from others' experiences and share your own, creating a collaborative environment.

Continuously Expanding Your Network

As you progress in your career, continue to expand your network. Repeat the cycle of attending events, meeting new people, and finding mentors who align with your evolving goals. Each stage of your career may require different types of guidance, and having a diverse network ensures you have the correct support at every step. Maintaining these connections long-term can provide ongoing benefits, including job referrals, collaborative opportunities, and a support system during career transitions.

Conclusion

Building professional relationships is a multifaceted process involving:

- Strategic networking

- Seeking and nurturing mentorship

- Maintaining effective communication

By actively engaging in these practices, you can accelerate your career progression, gain valuable support, and unlock new opportunities. Remember, the connections you make today can be the cornerstone of your success tomorrow.

Time is Your Most Valuable Asset: Prioritise What Truly Matters

Time is our most precious resource, and how we spend it significantly impacts our fulfilment and success. Prioritising time and focusing on what truly matters can lead to a more meaningful and satisfying life. As the ancient philosopher Seneca once said, ***"It is not that we have a short time to live, but that we waste a lot of it."*** This quote emphasises the importance of managing time wisely to achieve greater fulfilment.

The Importance of Valuing Time

1. **Enhanced Productivity**: Prioritising time helps focus on high-impact tasks, increasing productivity and efficiency.

2. **Improved Quality of Life**: Allocating time to activities that align with personal values and goals enhances overall well-being and satisfaction.

3. **Better Relationships**: Spending quality time with loved ones strengthens relationships and creates lasting memories.

4. **Personal Growth**: Dedicating time to learning and self-improvement fosters continuous growth and development.

5. **Achieving Goals**: Effective time management ensures progress towards personal and professional goals.

Strategies to Prioritise Time

1. **Set Clear Goals**: Define what you want to achieve in the short and long term. Clear goals provide direction and help prioritise tasks that align with your objectives.

    *   Set effective goals by using the SMART criteria (Specific, Measurable, Achievable, Relevant, and Time-bound).

2. **Create a Time Management Plan**: Schedule tasks and activities for your day, week, and month. A well-structured plan helps allocate time efficiently and prioritises important tasks.

    *   Tools like planners, calendars, and digital apps can help in organising your schedule.

3. **Prioritise Tasks**: Focus on tasks with the most significant impact. Use techniques like the Eisenhower Matrix to categorise tasks based on urgency and importance.

    *   Tackle high-priority tasks first and delegate or eliminate low-priority ones.

4. **Eliminate Time Wasters**: Identify activities that consume time without adding value and minimise or eliminate them. Common time wasters include excessive social media use, unnecessary meetings, and procrastination.

    *   Set specific times for checking emails and social media, and stick to them.

5. **Learn to Say No**: Respect your time by setting boundaries and learning to say no to tasks and commitments that do not align with your priorities.

   - Politely declining non-essential requests allows you to focus on what truly matters.

6. **Delegate Tasks**: Delegate tasks that others can handle. This frees up your time for high-priority activities that require your attention and expertise.

   - Effective delegation involves clear communication and trust in the abilities of others.

7. **Practise Mindfulness**: Stay present and focused on the task at hand. Mindfulness enhances concentration and reduces the tendency to get distracted.

   - Techniques such as meditation and deep breathing can improve mindfulness.

8. **Take Regular Breaks**: Incorporate breaks into your schedule to recharge and maintain productivity. Continuous work without breaks can lead to burnout and decreased efficiency.

   - The Pomodoro Technique, which involves working for 25 minutes followed by a 5-minute break, is an effective method.

9. **Reflect and Adjust**: Regularly review how you spend your time and make adjustments as needed. Reflection helps identify areas for improvement and ensures that your time aligns with your goals.

- Keep a time log to track activities and assess their value.

10. **Invest in Self-Care**: Prioritise activities that enhance your physical and mental well-being. Exercise, healthy eating, sufficient sleep, and relaxation are crucial for maintaining energy and focus.

- Schedule self-care activities just as you would schedule important work tasks.

Conclusion

Time is your most valuable asset, and prioritising how you spend it is essential for achieving fulfilment and success. Here are key strategies to make the most of your time and focus on what truly matters:

- Set clear goals
- Create a time management plan
- Prioritise tasks
- Eliminate time wasters
- Learn to say no
- Delegate tasks
- Practise mindfulness
- Take regular breaks
- Reflect and adjust
- Invest in self-care

Steve Jobs wisely noted, ***"Your time is limited, so don't waste it living someone else's life."*** Value your time, prioritise wisely, and lead a life that brings you true fulfilment and happiness.

Health is Wealth: Prioritising Physical and Mental Well-Being

The old adage "Health is wealth" holds timeless wisdom. Prioritising physical and mental health through regular exercise, a balanced diet, and stress management is fundamental to a fulfilling and productive life. As Mahatma Gandhi aptly said, ***"It is health that is real wealth and not pieces of gold and silver."*** This statement underscores the importance of maintaining good health to lead a rich and satisfying life.

The Importance of Prioritising Health

1. **Increased Productivity**: Good health enhances energy levels and concentration, improving productivity and efficiency.
2. **Better Quality of Life**: Physical and mental well-being contribute to overall happiness and life satisfaction.
3. **Reduced Healthcare Costs**: Maintaining good health can prevent chronic diseases and reduce the need for medical interventions, saving money in the long run.
4. **Longevity**: A healthy lifestyle promotes longevity and a higher quality of life in later years.
5. **Emotional Stability**: Good physical health supports mental health, promoting emotional balance and resilience.

Strategies to Prioritise Physical and Mental Health

1. **Regular Exercise**: Incorporate physical activity into your daily routine to improve cardiovascular health, strengthen muscles, and boost mental well-being.

   - Aim for at least 150 minutes of moderate aerobic activity or 75 minutes of vigorous activity per week, as recommended by the CDC.
   - Include a mix of cardio, strength training, and flexibility exercises for a well-rounded fitness routine.

2. **Balanced Diet**: Eat a balanced diet rich in fruits, vegetables, whole grains, lean proteins, and healthy fats to provide your body with essential nutrients.

   - Follow dietary guidelines such as the Mediterranean diet or DASH diet, which are known for their health benefits.
   - Limit processed foods, sugary drinks, and excessive salt and unhealthy fats.

3. **Adequate Sleep**: Prioritise sleep as an essential component of health. Aim for 7-9 hours of quality sleep per night to support physical and mental recovery.

   - Keep the bedroom cool, dark, and quiet to establish a regular sleep schedule and create a restful environment.
   - Avoid caffeine and electronic devices before bedtime to improve sleep quality.

4. **Stress Management**: Implement stress management techniques to maintain emotional balance and reduce the risk of stress-related illnesses.

   - Practise mindfulness, meditation, and deep breathing exercises to calm the mind and reduce stress.
   - Engage in hobbies and activities that bring joy and relaxation.

5. **Hydration**: Drink plenty of water throughout the day to stay hydrated and support overall health.

   - Aim for at least 8 cups (64 ounces) of water daily, more if you are active or live in a hot climate.
   - Monitor your hydration levels by checking the colour of your urine; light yellow indicates proper hydration.

6. **Regular Check-Ups**: Schedule regular medical check-ups and screenings to monitor your health and catch potential issues early.

   - Follow your doctor's recommendations for routine exams, vaccinations, and screenings based on your age and health history.
   - Stay informed about your health conditions and take proactive steps to manage them.

7. **Mental Health Care**: Prioritise mental health by seeking support when needed and practising self-care.

- Talk to a mental health professional if you experience anxiety, depression, or other mental health issues.
- Engage in activities that promote mental well-being, such as journaling, socialising, and pursuing creative outlets.

8. **Healthy Relationships**: Cultivate positive relationships with family, friends, and colleagues to support emotional well-being.

- Surround yourself with supportive and encouraging individuals.
- Communicate openly and resolve conflicts constructively to maintain healthy relationships.

9. **Limit Harmful Habits**: Avoid harmful habits such as smoking, excessive alcohol consumption, and drug use to protect your health.

- Seek support if you need help quitting smoking or reducing alcohol intake.
- Replace harmful habits with healthier alternatives, such as exercise or mindfulness practices.

10. **Stay Informed**: Educate yourself about health and wellness topics to make informed decisions about your lifestyle.

- Stay updated with reputable health information from sources like the CDC, WHO, and medical journals.

- Consult healthcare professionals for personalised advice and recommendations.

Conclusion

Prioritising physical and mental health through regular exercise, a balanced diet, and stress management is essential for a fulfilling and productive life. Here are key strategies to enhance your well-being and enjoy a higher quality of life:

- Regular exercise
- Balanced diet
- Stress management

By incorporating these into your daily routine, you can improve your well-being, reduce healthcare costs, and enjoy a higher quality of life. As Ralph Waldo Emerson wisely said, ***"The first wealth is health."*** Make health a priority, and you'll reap the benefits of a rich and satisfying life.

Pursue Your Passion: The Path to a Satisfying and Rewarding Life

Following what truly excites and motivates you is the key to living a more satisfying and rewarding life. Pursuing your passion brings joy and fulfilment and drives personal and professional success. As Steve Jobs famously said, ***"The only way to do great work is to love what you do."*** This statement highlights the profound impact of passion on achieving excellence and happiness.

The Importance of Pursuing Your Passion

1. **Increased Fulfilment**: Engaging in activities you are passionate about brings a deep sense of satisfaction and joy.
2. **Enhanced Motivation**: Passion fuels motivation, making overcoming challenges easier and staying committed to your goals.
3. **Improved Performance**: Doing what you love often leads to better performance, as you are likelier to put in the effort and dedication needed to excel.
4. **Personal Growth**: Pursuing your passion encourages continuous learning and development, leading to personal growth.
5. **Resilience**: Passion helps you stay resilient during tough times, as it provides a strong sense of purpose and direction.

Strategies to Pursue Your Passion

1. **Identify Your Passion**: Take time to reflect on what truly excites and motivates you. Consider your interests, hobbies, and the activities that make you lose track of time.

   - Journaling and self-reflection can help you identify your passions.
   - Ask yourself questions like, "What activities make me feel most alive?" and "What would I do if money were no object?"

2. **Set Clear Goals**: Once you've identified your passion, set clear and achievable goals to pursue it. Define both short-term and long-term objectives to guide your journey.

   - Set effective goals by using the SMART criteria (Specific, Measurable, Achievable, Relevant, and Time-bound).

3. **Take Action**: Start taking steps toward your passion, no matter how small. Taking action builds momentum and brings you closer to your goals.

   - Break down your goals into manageable tasks and tackle them one at a time.
   - Stay consistent and make pursuing your passion a regular part of your routine.

4. **Seek Support**: Surround yourself with supportive people encouraging and inspiring you to follow your

passion. Share your goals with friends, family, or mentors who can provide guidance and support.

- Join communities or groups related to your passion to connect with like-minded individuals.

5. **Embrace Lifelong Learning**: Continuously seek opportunities to learn and improve in your area of passion. Attend workshops, take courses, and read books to enhance your skills and knowledge.

- Stay curious and open to new experiences that can contribute to your growth.

6. **Stay Open to Change**: Be flexible and open to change as you pursue your passion. Sometimes, your interests and goals may evolve, and it's important to adapt and embrace new directions.

- Regularly reassess your goals and adjust your plans as needed.

7. **Balance Passion with Practicality**: While it's important to follow your passion, it's also essential to consider practical aspects such as financial stability. Find ways to balance your passion with your responsibilities.

- Consider pursuing your passion as a side project initially and gradually transitioning to it full-time.

8. **Persevere Through Challenges**: Pursuing your passion may come with challenges and setbacks. Stay resilient and keep pushing forward, even when faced with obstacles.

- Remember that setbacks are part of the journey and provide valuable learning experiences.

9. **Celebrate Progress**: Acknowledge and celebrate your achievements along the way. Recognising your progress boosts motivation and reinforces your commitment to your passion.

   - Celebrate both small milestones and major accomplishments.

10. **Maintain a Positive Mindset**: Cultivate a positive mindset and stay optimistic about your journey. Believing in yourself and your passion can make a significant difference in your success.

    - Practise gratitude and focus on the positive aspects of your journey.

Conclusion

Pursuing your passion leads to a more satisfying and rewarding life. Here are key steps to follow what truly excites and motivates you:

- Identify your passion
- Set clear goals
- Take action
- Seek support
- Embrace lifelong learning
- Stay open to change
- Balance passion with practicality
- Persevere through challenges

- Celebrate progress
- Maintain a positive mindset

As Oprah Winfrey wisely said, ***"Passion is energy. Feel the power that comes from focusing on what excites you."*** Follow your passion, and you will find both joy and success in your journey.

Practise Gratitude: The Key to Happiness and Resilience

Regularly acknowledging and appreciating the good in life fosters happiness and resilience. Practising gratitude helps shift focus from what is lacking to what is abundant, leading to a more positive outlook and increased emotional well-being. As Melody Beattie aptly stated, ***"Gratitude unlocks the fullness of life. It turns what we have into enough and more."*** This quote highlights the transformative power of gratitude.

The Importance of Practising Gratitude

1. **Enhanced Happiness**: Gratitude promotes a positive mindset, increasing overall happiness and life satisfaction.
2. **Improved Relationships**: Expressing gratitude strengthens relationships by fostering feelings of appreciation and connection.
3. **Greater Resilience**: Recognising the positives helps build emotional resilience, enabling you to cope better with challenges and setbacks.
4. **Better Physical Health**: Studies have shown that grateful people experience fewer aches and pains, better sleep, and overall improved health.
5. **Increased Mindfulness**: Practising gratitude encourages mindfulness and being present in the moment, enhancing daily experiences.

Strategies to Practise Gratitude

1. **Keep a Gratitude Journal**: Dedicate a few minutes each day to write down things you are grateful for. Reflecting on positive experiences can boost your mood and perspective.

   - Write about three to five things you are thankful for each day, no matter how small they may seem.

2. **Express Gratitude to Others**: Take time to thank the people in your life. Expressing appreciation strengthens relationships and spreads positivity.

   - Write thank-you notes, send appreciative messages, or verbally acknowledge someone's impact on your life.

3. **Practise Mindfulness**: Incorporate mindfulness practices into your daily routine to stay present and appreciate the moment.

   - Engage in activities such as meditation, deep breathing, or simply taking a moment to notice your surroundings and what you are grateful for.

4. **Reflect on Positive Experiences**: At the end of each day, reflect on your positive experiences. This practice helps reinforce a positive mindset and gratitude.

   - Consider what went well, moments of joy, or acts of kindness you witnessed or experienced.

5. **Create a Gratitude Ritual**: Establish a daily or weekly gratitude ritual to consistently practise appreciation.

- This could include sharing gratitude with family during meals, starting meetings with a moment of gratitude, or setting aside time each week to reflect on what you are thankful for.

6. **Use Visual Reminders**: Place visual reminders of gratitude around your home or workspace to prompt feelings of thankfulness.

    - Use sticky notes, pictures, or objects that symbolise things you are grateful for.

7. **Volunteer and Give Back**: Volunteering your time and resources to help others fosters gratitude by providing perspective and a sense of purpose.

    - Engage in community service, support charitable causes, or offer assistance to those in need.

8. **Focus on the Positive**: Make a conscious effort to focus on the positive aspects of your life and minimise dwelling on negatives.

    - Challenge negative thoughts by reframing them and identifying something positive in the situation.

9. **Celebrate Small Wins**: Acknowledge and celebrate small achievements and milestones. Recognising progress, no matter how minor, promotes gratitude.

    - Treat yourself or share your successes with others to reinforce positive feelings.

10. **Practise Self-Compassion**: Be kind to yourself and acknowledge your own efforts and achievements. Self-

compassion fosters internal gratitude and self-acceptance.

- Avoid self-criticism and practise positive self-talk, especially during challenging times.

Conclusion

Practising gratitude regularly leads to greater happiness and resilience. Here are key ways to cultivate a grateful mindset:

- Keep a gratitude journal
- Express gratitude to others
- Practise mindfulness
- Reflect on positive experiences
- Create a gratitude ritual
- Use visual reminders
- Volunteer
- Focus on the positive
- Celebrate small wins
- Practise self-compassion

As the Roman philosopher Cicero said, ***"Gratitude is not only the greatest of virtues but the parent of all others."*** Embrace gratitude, and you will unlock a richer, more fulfilling life filled with happiness and resilience.

Effective Communication is Key: Building Stronger Connections and Resolving Conflicts

Learning to communicate clearly and empathetically is crucial for resolving conflicts and building stronger connections. Effective communication fosters understanding, collaboration, and trust, essential components for both personal and professional relationships. As the American author and motivational speaker John C. Maxwell once said, **"People may hear your words, but they feel your attitude."** This highlights the importance of not just what we say, but how we say it.

The Importance of Effective Communication

1. **Conflict Resolution**: Clear and empathetic communication helps to address and resolve conflicts efficiently, minimising misunderstandings and fostering harmony.
2. **Stronger Relationships**: Effective communication builds trust and strengthens bonds, leading to more meaningful and supportive relationships.
3. **Enhanced Collaboration**: Good communication skills facilitate teamwork and collaboration, enabling individuals to work together more effectively.

4. **Increased Productivity**: Clear communication reduces errors and misunderstandings, leading to increased productivity and better outcomes.

5. **Personal Growth**: Developing communication skills enhances self-awareness and emotional intelligence, contributing to personal and professional growth.

Strategies to Communicate Effectively

1. **Listen Actively**: Focus on truly understanding the speaker's message without interrupting. Active listening shows respect and validates the speaker's perspective.

   - Use non-verbal cues like nodding and maintaining eye contact to show attentiveness.
   - Reflect back what you've heard by summarising or paraphrasing to ensure understanding.

2. **Be Clear and Concise**: Articulate your message clearly and concisely to avoid misunderstandings. Use simple language and be specific about your points.

   - Organise your thoughts before speaking and stick to the main points to maintain clarity.

3. **Show Empathy**: Empathy involves understanding and sharing the feelings of others. Show empathy by acknowledging emotions and validating concerns.

   - Use phrases like "I understand how you feel" or "That sounds challenging" to demonstrate empathy.

4. **Maintain Positive Body Language**: Non-verbal cues like posture, gestures, and facial expressions significantly impact communication. Maintain open and positive body language to reinforce your message.

   - Avoid crossing your arms or appearing distracted; instead, lean slightly forward and maintain a relaxed posture.

5. **Ask Questions**: Asking questions shows interest and encourages deeper conversation. It also helps clarify any doubts and ensures a mutual understanding.

   - Use open-ended questions to encourage detailed responses and gain more insights.

6. **Be Open and Honest**: Transparency fosters trust and credibility. Be honest in your communication and open to feedback and different perspectives.

   - Share your thoughts and feelings openly, and encourage others to do the same.

7. **Adapt to Your Audience**: Tailor your communication style to suit the needs and preferences of your audience. Consider factors like their background, knowledge level, and communication style.

   - Use appropriate language and examples that resonate with your audience.

8. **Provide Constructive Feedback**: Offer feedback that is specific, actionable, and focused on improvement.

Avoid criticising the person; instead, address the behaviour or issue.

- Use the "sandwich" method: start with a positive comment, provide constructive feedback, and end with a positive note.

9. **Practise Patience**: Effective communication often requires patience, especially in challenging situations. Take your time to listen, understand, and respond thoughtfully.

- Pause before responding to gather your thoughts and maintain a calm demeanour.

10. **Reflect and Improve**: Continuously reflect on your communication experiences and identify areas for improvement. Seek feedback from others to enhance your skills.

- Regularly practise and refine your communication techniques to become a more effective communicator.

Conclusion

Effective communication is key to resolving conflicts and building stronger connections. Here are essential strategies to enhance your communication skills:

- Listen actively
- Be clear and concise
- Show empathy
- Maintain positive body language

- Ask questions
- Be open and honest
- Adapt to your audience
- Provide constructive feedback
- Practise patience
- Reflect on your experiences

As Tony Robbins wisely said, ***"To effectively communicate, we must realise that we are all different in the way we perceive the world and use this understanding as a guide to our communication with others."*** Embrace these strategies, and you will create more meaningful and harmonious personal and professional relationships.

Live in the Present: Enhancing Life Quality by Focusing on the Now

Focusing on the present moment rather than dwelling on the past or worrying about the future significantly enhances the quality of life. Living in the present allows us to fully experience and appreciate each moment, leading to greater fulfilment and happiness. As the renowned spiritual teacher Eckhart Tolle said, ***"Realise deeply that the present moment is all you ever have. Make the Now the primary focus of your life."*** This wisdom emphasizes the importance of embracing the present to live a richer, more meaningful life.

The Importance of Living in the Present

1. **Enhanced Well-Being**: Living in the present reduces stress and anxiety associated with past regrets or future uncertainties.
2. **Greater Happiness**: Focusing on the current moment allows for a deeper appreciation of life's simple pleasures, increasing overall happiness.
3. **Improved Relationships**: Being present enhances interactions and connections with others, fostering stronger and more meaningful relationships.
4. **Increased Productivity**: Concentrating on the task at hand improves focus and efficiency, leading to better performance and productivity.

5. **Personal Growth**: Embracing the present moment fosters mindfulness and self-awareness, contributing to personal growth and development.

Strategies to Live in the Present

1. **Practise Mindfulness**: Engage in mindfulness exercises to cultivate awareness of the present moment. Mindfulness helps you stay focused and fully experience each moment.

    - Techniques such as meditation, deep breathing, and body scans can enhance mindfulness.

2. **Limit Distractions**: Minimise distractions that pull you away from the present. Turn off notifications, set boundaries for social media use, and create a focused environment.

    - Allocate specific times for checking emails and messages to avoid constant interruptions.

3. **Engage Your Senses**: Use your senses to ground yourself in the present moment. Notice the sights, sounds, smells, tastes, and textures around you.

    - Take a moment to Savour your food, listen to the sounds of nature, or feel the texture of an object.

4. **Let Go of the Past**: Release past regrets and negative experiences. Accept that the past cannot be changed and focus on what you can do now.

    - Practise forgiveness for yourself and others to let go of past burdens.

5. **Plan for the Future, but Don't Worry**: While planning for the future is important, avoid excessive worrying. Focus on what you can control and take proactive steps towards your goals.

   - Set realistic goals and break them down into manageable steps to reduce future-related anxiety.

6. **Practise Gratitude**: Regularly acknowledge and appreciate the positive aspects of your life. Gratitude shifts focus from what is lacking to what is abundant in the present.

   - Keep a gratitude journal and write down what you are thankful for daily.

7. **Accept Impermanence**: Recognise that everything is temporary and constantly changing. Embrace the present moment without clinging to it or fearing its end.

   - Appreciate the transient nature of experiences and find beauty in their impermanence.

8. **Engage Fully in Activities**: Immerse yourself in whatever you do. Whether it's work, hobbies, or spending time with loved ones, give your complete attention to the activity.

   - Practise single-tasking instead of multitasking to enhance focus and enjoyment.

9. **Develop a Positive Mindset**: Cultivate a positive attitude towards the present moment. Focus on the

good aspects of your current situation and find joy in the here and now.

- Practise positive affirmations and focus on solutions rather than problems.

10. **Seek Professional Help if Needed**: If you find it challenging to stay present due to anxiety or past trauma, seek support from a mental health professional.

- Therapy can provide tools and strategies to help you live more fully in the present.

Conclusion

Living in the present moment enhances life quality by reducing stress, increasing happiness, improving relationships, boosting productivity, and fostering personal growth. Here are key strategies to cultivate the habit of living in the present:

- Practise mindfulness
- Limit distractions
- Engage your senses
- Let go of the past
- Plan for the future without worrying
- Practise gratitude
- Accept impermanence
- Engage fully in activities
- Develop a positive mindset
- Seek professional help if needed

As Buddha wisely said, "Do not dwell in the past, do not dream of the future, concentrate the mind on the present moment." Embrace the present, and you will find greater joy, fulfilment, and peace in your life.

Be Open to Change: Embracing Adaptability for Growth

Embracing change and being adaptable is crucial for personal and professional growth. The ability to navigate and thrive in changing environments opens doors to new opportunities and enhances resilience. As Charles Darwin famously stated, ***"It is not the strongest of the species that survive, nor the most intelligent, but the one most responsive to change."*** This quote highlights the importance of adaptability in achieving success and growth.

The Importance of Embracing Change

1. **Personal Growth**: Change challenges you to step out of your comfort zone, fostering personal development and self-discovery.

2. **Professional Advancement**: Being adaptable makes you more valuable in the workplace, opening up career progression and success opportunities.

3. **Increased Resilience**: Embracing change helps build resilience, enabling you to effectively handle setbacks and challenges.

4. **Enhanced Creativity**: Adaptability encourages innovative thinking and creative problem-solving, essential skills in today's dynamic world.

5. **Broader Perspectives**: Experiencing change exposes you to new ideas, cultures, and ways of thinking, broadening your horizons and understanding.

Strategies to Embrace Change

1. **Adopt a Growth Mindset**: Believe in your ability to grow and adapt. A growth mindset helps you see change as an opportunity for learning and improvement.

    - Carol Dweck's book "Mindset: The New Psychology of Success" explores the concept of a growth mindset and its benefits.

2. **Stay Curious and Open-Minded**: Cultivate curiosity and openness to new experiences and perspectives. Being willing to learn and explore makes it easier to adapt to change.

    - Ask questions, seek out new experiences, and stay informed about trends and developments in your field.

3. **Develop Flexibility**: Practise being flexible in your thinking and actions. Flexibility allows you to adjust your plans and strategies when faced with unexpected changes.

    - Practise problem-solving and decision-making in various scenarios to enhance your flexibility.

4. **Embrace Uncertainty**: Accept that change often brings uncertainty. Embracing uncertainty reduces anxiety and helps you navigate new situations with confidence.

    - Focus on what you can control and take proactive steps to manage uncertainty.

5. **Build a Support Network**: Surround yourself with supportive people who encourage adaptability and growth. A strong support network provides guidance and reassurance during times of change.

   - Seek out mentors, colleagues, and friends who have experience with adapting to change.

6. **Learn Continuously**: Commit to lifelong learning. Continuous education and skill development keep you prepared for changing circumstances and new opportunities.

   - Take courses, attend workshops, and read widely to stay updated and knowledgeable.

7. **Practise Resilience**: Develop resilience by embracing challenges and learning from setbacks. Resilience helps you bounce back stronger from difficult situations.

   - Engage in activities that build mental and emotional strength, such as mindfulness and stress management practices.

8. **Set Realistic Goals**: Set achievable goals that allow you to adapt to change incrementally. Breaking down larger changes into smaller, manageable steps makes them less overwhelming.

   - Set effective goals by using the SMART criteria (Specific, Measurable, Achievable, Relevant, and Time-bound).

9. **Reflect and Adapt**: Regularly reflect on your experiences and adapt your approach as needed. Reflection helps you learn from past changes and improve your adaptability.

- Keep a journal to document your thoughts, challenges, and strategies for adapting to change.

10. **Celebrate Adaptability**: Recognise and celebrate your ability to adapt and grow. Acknowledging your successes reinforces a positive attitude towards change.

- Share your achievements with others and take pride in your adaptability.

Conclusion

Being open to change and embracing adaptability are essential for personal and professional growth. Here are key strategies to help you navigate change with confidence and thrive in evolving environments:

- Adopt a growth mindset
- Stay curious and open-minded
- Develop flexibility
- Embrace uncertainty
- Build a support network
- Learn continuously
- Practise resilience
- Set realistic goals
- Reflect and adapt
- Celebrate adaptability

As Heraclitus wisely noted, ***"The only constant in life is change."*** Embrace change, and you will unlock new opportunities for growth and success.

Life-Changing Lessons I Learned Too Late:
Wisdom, I wish I had Known At My First Job

As Heraclitus wisely noted, ***"The only constant in life is change."*** Embrace change, and you will unlock new opportunities for growth and success.

Page | 93

Learn to Say No: Setting Boundaries for a Healthier Balance

Learning to say no is crucial for maintaining a healthy balance and focusing on priorities. Setting boundaries and not overcommitting ensures that you can dedicate your time and energy to what truly matters. As Warren Buffett wisely stated, ***"The difference between successful people and really successful people is that really successful people say no to almost everything."*** This highlights the importance of selectively committing to tasks and responsibilities to achieve success and well-being.

The Importance of Learning to Say No

1. **Enhanced Focus**: Saying no to non-essential tasks allows you to concentrate on your most important goals and priorities.
2. **Reduced Stress**: Setting boundaries helps prevent overcommitment and the resulting stress and burnout.
3. **Improved Productivity**: Focusing on fewer tasks enables you to perform better and achieve higher quality outcomes.
4. **Better Work-Life Balance**: Saying no ensures you have time for personal activities, relationships, and self-care.
5. **Increased Self-Respect**: Setting boundaries and prioritising your needs fosters self-respect and self-worth.

Strategies to Learn to Say No

1. **Know Your Priorities**: Clearly define your priorities and goals. Understanding what is most important to you makes it easier to decide when to say no.

   - Write down your top priorities and refer to them when evaluating new commitments.

2. **Be Honest and Direct**: When you need to say no, be honest and direct about your reasons. Avoid vague excuses and clearly communicate your limitations.

   - Use statements like, "I appreciate the opportunity, but I need to focus on my current commitments."

3. **Practise Assertiveness**: Develop assertiveness to say no without feeling guilty or pressured confidently. Assertiveness helps you set boundaries respectfully and effectively.

- Practise assertive communication techniques, such as using "I" statements and maintaining eye contact.

4. **Offer Alternatives**: When appropriate, offer alternatives or suggest someone else who might be able to help. This shows that you are considerate while still maintaining your boundaries.

   - For example, "I can't take this on right now, but perhaps [Name] could assist you."

5. **Evaluate Requests Carefully**: Take time to evaluate requests before responding. Consider how the commitment aligns with your priorities and whether you have the capacity to take it on.

- Use a decision-making framework, such as the Eisenhower Matrix, to assess the urgency and importance of the request.

6. **Set Clear Boundaries**: Establish clear boundaries for your time and energy. Communicate these boundaries to others to manage expectations.

   - Let colleagues and friends know your availability and limits to prevent over-commitment.

7. **Practise Saying No**: Build confidence by practising saying no in low-stakes situations. The more you practise, the more comfortable you will become with setting boundaries.

   - Role-play scenarios with a friend or family member to strengthen your ability to say no.

8. **Prioritise Self-Care**: Recognise that taking care of yourself is a valid reason to say no. Prioritising self-care ensures you have the energy and well-being to meet your commitments.

   - Schedule regular self-care activities and treat them as non-negotiable appointments.

9. **Learn to Delegate**: Delegate tasks, when possible, to lighten your workload. Trusting others to handle responsibilities can free up your time for higher-priority activities.

   - Identify tasks that can be delegated and find suitable individuals to take them on.

10. **Reflect on Past Experiences**: Reflect on times when you overcommitted and the impact it had on your well-being. Use these experiences to reinforce the importance of setting boundaries.

- Keep a journal to document your reflections and lessons learned from over-commitment.

Conclusion

Learning to say no is essential for setting boundaries, maintaining a healthy balance, and focusing on priorities. Here are key strategies to help you confidently set boundaries and manage your commitments effectively:

- Know your priorities
- Be honest and direct
- Practise assertiveness
- Offer alternatives
- Evaluate requests carefully
- Set clear boundaries
- Practise saying no
- Prioritise self-care
- Learn to delegate
- Reflect on past experiences

As Steve Jobs famously said, ***"It's only by saying no that you can concentrate on the really important things."*** Embrace the power of saying no, and you will achieve greater focus, balance, and success in your life.

Seek Help When Needed: A Step Towards Growth and Problem-Solving

Asking for help and seeking support is not a sign of weakness; it is a crucial step toward growth and effective problem-solving. Recognising when you need assistance and taking action to obtain it can lead to personal and professional development, improved mental health, and better outcomes. As former First Lady Michelle Obama wisely said, ***"Asking for help is always a sign of strength."*** Embracing this mindset empowers you to overcome challenges and achieve your goals more effectively.

The Importance of Seeking Help

1. **Enhanced Problem-Solving**: Seeking help provides new perspectives and insights, enabling you to tackle challenges more effectively.
2. **Personal Growth**: Asking for assistance fosters learning and development, helping you acquire new skills and knowledge.
3. **Improved Mental Health**: Sharing your burdens and receiving support can alleviate stress, anxiety, and feelings of isolation.
4. **Strengthened Relationships**: Reaching out for help builds trust and deepens connections with others, fostering a supportive network.
5. **Increased Efficiency**: Collaborating with others can streamline tasks and lead to more efficient and successful outcomes.

Strategies to Seek Help Effectively

1. **Recognise When You Need Help**: Be aware of your limitations and acknowledge when you need assistance. Self-awareness is the first step toward seeking support.

   - Reflect on your workload, stress levels, and areas where you feel stuck or overwhelmed.

2. **Identify the Right Resources**: Determine who or what can best provide the help you need. This could be a mentor, colleague, friend, or professional service.

   - Consider the expertise, experience, and availability of the person or resource you plan to approach.

3. **Communicate Clearly**: When asking for help, be specific about what you need. Clear communication ensures that you receive the appropriate support.

   - Explain the situation, outline your challenges, and specify the type of assistance you are seeking.

4. **Be Open and Honest**: Share your struggles openly and honestly. Transparency fosters trust and enables others to provide more effective support.

   - Don't downplay your difficulties; instead, articulate your concerns and their impact.

5. **Show Appreciation**: Express gratitude to those who offer their help and support. Acknowledging their assistance strengthens relationships and encourages future collaboration.

- A simple thank-you note or verbal acknowledgement can go a long way in showing appreciation.

6. **Follow Through** Act on the advice and assistance you receive. Following through demonstrates that you value the help and are committed to solving the problem.

   - Implement the suggestions and provide updates to those who helped you.

7. **Build a Support Network**: Cultivate a network of trusted individuals who can offer support and guidance when needed. A strong support system provides a safety net during challenging times.

   - Engage with mentors, join professional groups, and maintain close relationships with friends and family.

8. **Offer Help in Return**: Be willing to help others when they need support. Reciprocity strengthens relationships and builds a culture of mutual assistance.

   - Actively listen, provide advice, and offer your skills to help others succeed.

9. **Seek Professional Help When Needed**: Don't hesitate to seek professional help for complex issues. Therapists, counsellors, and consultants can provide specialised support.

   - Recognise when a problem requires professional expertise and take action to get the necessary help.

10. **Reflect and Learn**: After receiving help, reflect on the experience and what you learned. Use these insights to improve your problem-solving skills and grow.

- Consider how the support helped you and how you can apply these lessons in the future.

Conclusion

Seeking help when needed is a sign of strength and a step toward growth and effective problem-solving. Here are key strategies to help you navigate challenges more effectively and achieve your goals:

- Recognise when you need assistance
- Identify the right resources
- Communicate clearly
- Be open and honest
- Show appreciation
- Follow through
- Build a support network
- Offer help in return
- Seek professional help when needed
- Reflect and learn

As Helen Keller once said, ***"Alone we can do so little; together we can do so much."*** Embrace the power of seeking help, and you will find greater strength, resilience, and success in your personal and professional life.

Mindfulness and Meditation: Reducing Stress and Improving Mental Clarity

Practising mindfulness and meditation can significantly reduce stress and improve mental clarity, leading to a more balanced and fulfilling life. These practices cultivate a sense of presence and awareness, helping you navigate the complexities of daily life with greater ease and focus. As Jon Kabat-Zinn, the pioneer of mindfulness-based stress reduction, said, ***"Mindfulness is a way of befriending ourselves and our experience."*** Embracing mindfulness and meditation can transform your mental and emotional well-being.

The Importance of Mindfulness and Meditation

1. **Stress Reduction**: Mindfulness and meditation help lower stress levels by promoting relaxation and reducing the physiological impacts of stress.
2. **Improved Mental Clarity**: These practices enhance focus and concentration, leading to better decision-making and productivity.
3. **Emotional Regulation**: Mindfulness and meditation foster emotional stability, helping you manage your reactions and maintain calm in challenging situations.
4. **Enhanced Self-Awareness**: Practising mindfulness increases self-awareness, enabling you to understand your thoughts, emotions, and behaviours more deeply.

5. **Better Health**: Regular meditation can improve overall health, including better sleep, lower blood pressure, and reduced symptoms of anxiety and depression.

Strategies to Practise Mindfulness and Meditation

1. **Start with Breath Awareness**: Begin your mindfulness practice by focusing on your breath. Pay attention to the sensation of breathing in and out, which helps anchor you in the present moment.

   - Spend a few minutes each day sitting quietly and observing your breath.

2. **Set Aside Time Daily**: Dedicate a specific time each day for mindfulness and meditation practice. Consistency is key to experiencing the benefits.

   - Start with short sessions of 5-10 minutes and gradually increase the duration as you become more comfortable.

3. **Create a Quiet Space**: Find a quiet and comfortable place where you can practise without distractions. A peaceful environment enhances your ability to focus and relax.

   - Sit comfortably on a cushion or chair, and consider using a timer to record your session.

4. **Use Guided Meditations**: Guided meditations can be helpful, especially for beginners. These sessions provide structure and guidance, making it easier to stay focused.

- Apps like Headspace, Calm, and Insight Timer offer a wide range of guided meditations for different needs and preferences.

5. **Practise Mindful Walking**: Incorporate mindfulness into your daily activities, such as walking. Pay attention to the sensation of your feet touching the ground, the movement of your body, and the sights and sounds around you.

   - Take a few minutes daily to walk mindfully, focusing on the present moment.

6. **Body Scan Meditation**: Practise body scan meditation to develop awareness of physical sensations. This technique involves systematically focusing on different parts of your body, from head to toe.

   - Lie down or sit comfortably, and mentally scan your body, noticing any tension or discomfort.

7. **Mindful Eating**: Bring mindfulness to your meals by paying full attention to the experience of eating. Notice your food's Flavors, textures, and smells, and eat slowly and deliberately.

   - Turn off distractions like TV or smartphones during meals to fully engage in mindful eating.

8. **Practise Gratitude**: Incorporate gratitude into your mindfulness practice by reflecting on things you are thankful for. This enhances positive emotions and overall well-being.

- Spend a few minutes each day thinking about or writing down things you are grateful for.

9. **Observe Your Thoughts**: Observe your thoughts without judgment during meditation. Notice them as they come and go, and gently bring your focus back to your breath or chosen point of focus.

   - Recognise that it's natural for the mind to wander and gently refocus without frustration.

10. **Join a Meditation Group**: Practising with others can provide support and encouragement. Join a local meditation group or online community to share experiences and deepen your practice.

    - Participating in group sessions or workshops can enhance your commitment and provide valuable insights.

Conclusion

Mindfulness and meditation are powerful tools for reducing stress and improving mental clarity. Here are key strategies to cultivate mindfulness and reap its numerous benefits:

- Start with breath awareness
- Set aside daily practice time
- Create a quiet space
- Use guided meditations
- Practise mindful walking and eating
- Perform body scan meditations
- Incorporate gratitude

- Observe thoughts
- Join a meditation group

As the Buddha wisely said, ***"The mind is everything. What you think, you become."*** Embrace mindfulness and meditation to foster a peaceful, focused, and resilient mind.

Value Experiences Over Material Goods:

Enriching Life Through Memories

Memories and experiences enrich life far more than accumulating material possessions. While material goods may provide temporary satisfaction, experiences create lasting memories, foster personal growth, and bring deeper fulfilment. As the Dalai Lama wisely stated, ***"Happiness is not something ready-made. It comes from your own actions."*** Emphasising experiences over material goods can lead to a richer, more meaningful life.

The Importance of Valuing Experiences

1. **Lasting Happiness**: Experiences provide enduring happiness and satisfaction, while the joy from material possessions often fades quickly.
2. **Personal Growth**: Engaging in new activities and exploring different places encourages learning and personal development.
3. **Stronger Relationships**: Shared experiences strengthen bonds with friends and family, creating meaningful connections.
4. **Enhanced Well-Being**: Participating in enriching activities boosts mental and emotional well-being.
5. **Life Enrichment**: Experiences add depth and variety to life, making it more interesting and fulfilling.

Strategies to Value Experiences Over Material Goods

1. **Prioritise Travel and Exploration**: Invest in travel and exploration to discover new cultures, landscapes, and perspectives. Traveling broadens your horizons and creates unforgettable memories.

   - Plan trips to places you've always wanted to visit, whether near or far, and immerse yourself in the local culture.

2. **Engage in Hobbies and Interests**: Pursue hobbies and interests that bring you joy and fulfilment. Engaging in activities you love enriches your life and provides a sense of accomplishment.

   - Take up new hobbies or revisit old ones, such as painting, hiking, cooking, or playing an instrument.

3. **Spend Quality Time with Loved Ones**: Focus on spending quality time with family and friends. Shared experiences, like family outings or game nights, create cherished memories.

   - Plan regular gatherings, outings, or activities that you can enjoy together.

4. **Invest in Learning and Skill Development**: Allocate resources to learning new skills or furthering your education. Investing in yourself through courses, workshops, or personal projects leads to personal and professional growth.

   - Enrol in classes that interest you, attend seminars, or take up a new craft.

5. **Participate in Events and Activities**: Attend concerts, theatre performances, sports events, and community activities. These experiences provide entertainment and a sense of community.

   - Look for local events and activities that align with your interests and make a point to participate.

6. **Create Traditions and Rituals**: Establish traditions and rituals that bring meaning and joy to your life. Celebrating holidays, milestones, and personal achievements with unique rituals creates lasting memories.

   - Create your own family traditions or participate in cultural and community rituals.

7. **Practise Mindfulness**: Be present and fully engage in your experiences. Mindfulness helps you appreciate and savour each moment, enhancing the value of your experiences.

   - Incorporate mindfulness practices like meditation, deep breathing, or simply paying full attention to the present moment.

8. **Document Your Experiences**: Capture and document your experiences through photos, journals, or scrapbooks. Reflecting on these memories reinforces their value and brings joy.

   - Keep a travel journal, create photo albums, or write about your experiences in a blog.

9. **Give Experience-Based Gifts**: Instead of material gifts, give the gift of experiences to others. Tickets to events, vouchers for activities, or planned outings can create lasting joy and memories.

   - Consider gifting experiences such as a cooking class, a spa day, or a weekend getaway.

10. **Live Simply**: Simplify your life by reducing the emphasis on material possessions. Focus on what truly brings you joy and fulfilment.

    - Declutter your living space, prioritise meaningful activities, and avoid unnecessary purchases.

Conclusion

Valuing experiences over material goods leads to a richer, more fulfilling life. Here are key ways to enrich your life with lasting memories and personal growth:

- Prioritise travel and exploration
- Engage in hobbies
- Spend quality time with loved ones
- Invest in learning
- Participate in events
- Create traditions
- Practise mindfulness
- Document experiences
- Give experience-based gifts
- Live simply

As Albert Einstein said**, "The only source of knowledge is experience."** Embrace experiences to find deeper happiness and a more meaningful existence.

Life-Changing Lessons I Learned Too Late:
Wisdom, I wish I had Known At My First Job

As Albert Einstein said**, "The only source of knowledge is experience."** Embrace experiences to find deeper happiness and a more meaningful existence.

Develop a Growth Mindset: Unlocking Potential Through Effort and Persistence

Believing in the ability to grow and learn through effort and persistence is transformative. Developing a growth mindset—an understanding that abilities and intelligence can be developed with time and effort—can lead to remarkable personal and professional growth. As a leading researcher in motivation and development, Carol Dweck said*, "The view you adopt for yourself profoundly affects the way you lead your life."* Embracing a growth mindset unlocks potential and fosters resilience, creativity, and a love for learning.

The Importance of a Growth Mindset

1. **Enhanced Learning**: A growth mindset encourages continuous learning and improvement, leading to the acquisition of new skills and knowledge.
2. **Resilience**: Believing in the ability to grow fosters resilience, enabling individuals to bounce back from setbacks and challenges.
3. **Increased Motivation**: A growth mindset fuels motivation and drive, as individuals understand that effort leads to improvement.
4. **Greater Achievement**: Embracing a growth mindset can lead to higher levels of achievement and success in various areas of life.

5. **Improved Relationships**: A growth mindset promotes open-mindedness and empathy, enhancing personal and professional relationships.

Strategies to Develop a Growth Mindset

1. **Embrace Challenges**: View challenges as opportunities to learn and grow rather than obstacles. Embracing challenges helps develop problem-solving skills and resilience.

   - Take on tasks that stretch your abilities and push you out of your comfort zone.

2. **Learn from Criticism**: Use constructive criticism as a tool for improvement. Feedback provides valuable insights into areas where you can grow.

   - Listen to feedback with an open mind and take actionable steps to address areas for improvement.

3. **Celebrate Effort**: Focus on the effort rather than the outcome. Recognise and celebrate the hard work and perseverance you put into tasks.

   - Praise yourself and others for effort, persistence, and improvement rather than just results.

4. **Adopt a Positive Attitude**: Maintain a positive attitude towards learning and growth. Believe that your abilities can be developed with time and effort.

   - Replace negative self-talk with positive affirmations and focus on progress rather than perfection.

5. **Set Learning Goals**: Set specific, measurable goals focused on learning and development. Clear goals provide direction and motivation.

   - Use the SMART criteria (Specific, Measurable, Achievable, Relevant, Time-bound) to set effective learning goals.

6. **Persevere Through Difficulties**: Stay committed and persistent, even when faced with difficulties. Understand that setbacks are a natural part of the learning process.

   - Develop strategies to stay motivated, such as breaking tasks into smaller steps and rewarding yourself for progress.

7. **Cultivate Curiosity**: Foster a curious mindset by seeking out new experiences, asking questions, and exploring different perspectives.

   - Engage in activities that stimulate your curiosity and encourage you to learn something new every day.

8. **Practise Self-Reflection**: Regularly reflect on your experiences and progress. Self-reflection helps identify areas for growth and reinforces a growth mindset.

   - Keep a journal to document your reflections, challenges, and achievements.

9. **Surround Yourself with Growth-Minded Individuals**: Build a network of supportive, growth-minded individuals who encourage and inspire you.

- Seek out mentors, join communities, and engage with people who share a commitment to growth and learning.

10. **Focus on the Process**: Concentrate on the learning process rather than the end result. Enjoy the journey of growth and improvement.

- Engage fully in the tasks at hand and appreciate the learning and development that occur along the way.

Conclusion

Developing a growth mindset is transformative, unlocking potential and fostering continuous learning, resilience, and achievement. Here are key strategies to cultivate a growth mindset:

- Embrace challenges
- Learn from criticism
- Celebrate effort
- Adopt a positive attitude
- Set learning goals
- Persevere through difficulties
- Cultivate curiosity
- Practise self-reflection
- Surround yourself with growth-minded individuals
- Focus on the process

As Carol Dweck emphasised, ***"Becoming is better than being."*** Embrace the journey of growth and learning, and you will achieve greater success and fulfilment in all areas of life.

Patience is Powerful: The Key to Reducing Frustration and Enhancing Decision-Making

Understanding that good things often take time is a powerful mindset that can significantly reduce frustration and improve decision-making. Patience allows you to approach challenges calmly and measuredly, leading to more thoughtful and effective outcomes. As the famous saying goes, "Patience is not the ability to wait, but the ability to keep a good attitude while waiting." Embracing patience can transform how you handle life's ups and downs, ultimately leading to greater success and satisfaction.

The Importance of Patience

1. **Reduced Frustration**: Patience helps manage expectations and reduces frustration when things don't happen as quickly as desired.
2. **Better Decision-Making**: Considering all options and outcomes leads to more informed and effective decisions.
3. **Enhanced Resilience**: Patience builds resilience, enabling you to withstand setbacks and persist through challenges.
4. **Improved Relationships**: Patience fosters empathy and understanding, strengthening personal and professional relationships.

5. **Increased Success**: Many successful outcomes require time and sustained effort. Patience ensures you stay committed to your goals.

Strategies to Cultivate Patience

1. **Practise Mindfulness**: Engage in mindfulness exercises to stay present and focused. Mindfulness reduces impatience by encouraging a calm and centred mindset.

   - Techniques such as deep breathing, meditation, and yoga can help cultivate mindfulness.

2. **Set Realistic Expectations**: Recognise that achieving significant goals often takes time. Set realistic timelines and be prepared for delays or obstacles.

   - Break down large goals into smaller, manageable steps to make progress feel more attainable.

3. **Focus on the Process**: Enjoy the journey rather than just the destination. Focusing on the process and the small steps along the way can make the wait more bearable.

   - Celebrate small milestones and appreciate the progress you make each day.

4. **Develop a Long-Term Perspective**: Look at the big picture and understand that short-term setbacks are part of the journey to long-term success.

   - Remind yourself of your ultimate goals and the reasons behind them to maintain motivation.

5. **Learn from Waiting**: Use waiting periods as opportunities to learn and grow. Patience provides time for reflection and self-improvement.

   - Engage in productive activities or hobbies while waiting to maximise your time.

6. **Practise Self-Compassion**: Be kind to yourself during times of waiting and uncertainty. Self-compassion reduces the stress and frustration associated with impatience.

   - Treat yourself with the same understanding and patience you would offer a friend.

7. **Embrace Delays**: View delays and obstacles as opportunities to reassess and improve your plans. Embracing delays helps maintain a positive attitude.

   - Use delays as a chance to gather more information, refine your approach, or explore alternative options.

8. **Stay Positive**: Maintain a positive outlook and focus on the benefits of patience. A positive attitude helps you stay motivated and resilient.

   - Practise gratitude and focus on the good things in your life to foster a positive mindset.

9. **Seek Support**: Surround yourself with supportive people who encourage patience and perseverance. A strong support network provides encouragement and perspective.

- Share your goals and challenges with friends, family, or mentors who can offer guidance and support.

10. **Reflect on Past Successes**: Recall times when patience paid off in the past. Reflecting on previous successes reinforces the value of patience.

- Keep a journal of past achievements and the patience it took to attain them to remind yourself of the benefits.

Conclusion

Patience is a powerful tool that reduces frustration and improves decision-making. Here are key strategies to cultivate patience and harness its benefits:

- Practise mindfulness
- Set realistic expectations
- Focus on the process
- Develop a long-term perspective
- Learn from waiting
- Practise self-compassion
- Embrace delays
- Stay positive
- Seek support
- Reflect on past successes

As Lao Tzu wisely said, ***"Nature does not hurry, yet everything is accomplished."*** Embrace patience, and you will find greater peace, resilience, and success in your personal and professional life.

Practise Self-Compassion: Fostering Resilience and Well-Being

Being kind to oneself during tough times fosters resilience and well-being. Practising self-compassion involves treating yourself with the same kindness, understanding, and support that you would offer a friend. This approach can significantly enhance your emotional health and ability to navigate challenges. As Kristin Neff, a pioneer in self-compassion research, said, "When we give ourselves compassion, we are opening our hearts in a way that can transform our lives." Embracing self-compassion can transform the way you experience and respond to difficulties.

The Importance of Self-Compassion

1. **Enhanced Resilience**: Self-compassion builds resilience, enabling you to bounce back from setbacks and adversity with greater strength.
2. **Improved Mental Health**: Being kind to yourself reduces stress, anxiety, and depression, contributing to better overall mental health.
3. **Increased Self-Esteem**: Practising self-compassion fosters a positive self-image and boosts self-esteem.
4. **Better Decision-Making**: Self-compassion allows for clearer thinking and better decision-making by reducing the negative impact of self-criticism.

5. **Greater Life Satisfaction**: Self-compassion enhances overall well-being and life satisfaction by promoting a healthier, more positive outlook.

Strategies to Practise Self-Compassion

1. **Acknowledge Your Feelings**: Recognise and accept your emotions without judgment. Validating your feelings is the first step toward self-compassion.

   - Allow yourself to feel without immediately trying to change or fix your emotions.

2. **Speak Kindly to Yourself**: Replace self-critical thoughts with kind and supportive self-talk. Treat yourself with the same empathy you would offer a friend.

   - Use affirmations and positive statements to counter negative self-talk.

3. **Practise Mindfulness**: Engage in mindfulness to stay present and aware of your experiences without judgment. Mindfulness helps you observe your thoughts and emotions with compassion.

   - Techniques like meditation, deep breathing, and body scans can enhance mindfulness.

4. **Understand Common Humanity**: Everyone experiences difficulties and makes mistakes. Understanding that you are not alone in your struggles fosters a sense of connection and compassion.

   - Remind yourself that imperfection is part of the human experience.

5. **Take Care of Your Needs**: Prioritise self-care and ensure your physical, emotional, and mental needs are met. Taking care of yourself is a fundamental aspect of self-compassion.

   - Engage in activities that nourish and rejuvenate you, such as exercise, hobbies, and rest.

6. **Practise Self-Forgiveness**: Forgive yourself for past mistakes and let go of guilt and shame. Self-forgiveness is essential for moving forward with compassion.

   - Reflect on your mistakes, learn from them, and then release any lingering self-blame.

7. **Set Healthy Boundaries**: Establish boundaries that protect your well-being. Saying no to excessive demands and respecting your limits is an act of self-compassion.

   - Communicate your boundaries clearly and assertively to others.

8. **Reflect on Your Strengths**: Focus on your strengths and accomplishments. Acknowledging your positive qualities fosters a compassionate and appreciative self-view.

   - Keep a journal of your achievements and strengths to reinforce a positive self-image.

9. **Seek Support**: Reach out for support from friends, family, or professionals when needed. Asking for help is

an act of self-compassion and can provide valuable perspective and encouragement.

- Don't hesitate to seek therapy or counselling if you need additional support.

10. **Practise Gratitude**: Cultivate gratitude by regularly reflecting on the positive aspects of your life. Gratitude enhances well-being and encourages a compassionate mindset.

- Write down things you are grateful for each day and reflect on the good moments.

Conclusion

Practising self-compassion is essential for fostering resilience and well-being. Here are key strategies to develop a compassionate relationship with yourself:

- Acknowledge your feelings
- Speak kindly to yourself
- Practise mindfulness
- Understand common humanity
- Take care of your needs
- Practise self-forgiveness
- Set healthy boundaries
- Reflect on your strengths
- Seek support
- Practise gratitude

Buddha wisely said, ***"You yourself, as much as anybody in the universe, deserve your love and affection."*** Embrace self-compassion, and you will find greater strength, peace, and fulfilment in your life.

Cultivate Empathy: Strengthening Relationships and Building Community

Cultivating empathy—understanding and sharing the feelings of others—is essential for strengthening relationships and building a supportive community. Empathy fosters connection, compassion, and mutual respect, creating a foundation for meaningful interactions and collaborative efforts. As renowned author and researcher Brené Brown said, ***"Empathy is feeling with people."*** Embracing empathy can transform how we relate to others and enhance our social bonds.

The Importance of Empathy

1. **Enhanced Relationships**: Empathy deepens understanding and trust, strengthening personal and professional relationships.
2. **Improved Communication**: Empathetic communication fosters openness and reduces misunderstandings.
3. **Conflict Resolution**: Understanding others' perspectives helps in resolving conflicts more effectively and harmoniously.
4. **Emotional Support**: Empathy provides emotional support, showing others that they are not alone in their struggles.
5. **Community Building**: Empathy fosters a sense of belonging and solidarity, creating a more compassionate and cohesive community.

Strategies to Cultivate Empathy

1. **Active Listening**: Listen attentively to others without interrupting. Active listening involves fully engaging with the speaker, showing interest, and reflecting back on what you hear.

    - Use verbal and nonverbal cues, such as nodding and maintaining eye contact, to show that you are listening.

2. **Ask Open-Ended Questions**: Encourage others to share their feelings and experiences by asking open-ended questions. This shows that you value their perspective and are interested in understanding them.

    - Use questions like "How did that make you feel?" or "Can you tell me more about your experience?"

3. **Validate Feelings**: Acknowledge and validate the emotions of others. Let them know that their feelings are understood and accepted.

    - Use phrases like "I can see why you feel that way" or "That sounds really challenging."

4. **Practise Perspective-Taking**: Try to put yourself in others' shoes and see the situation from their point of view. Perspective-taking enhances your ability to understand and empathize with their feelings.

    - Reflect on how you would feel in a similar situation and consider the factors influencing their perspective.

5. **Show Compassion**: Respond to others with kindness and compassion. Offering support and understanding strengthens your connection and demonstrates empathy.

   - Small acts of kindness, such as offering a listening ear or a comforting word, can make a significant impact.

6. **Be Present**: Give your full attention to others during interactions. Being present shows that you value their time and feelings.

   - Minimise distractions, such as turning off your phone or stepping away from your computer, during conversations.

7. **Share Your Own Feelings**: Open up about your own emotions and experiences. Sharing your feelings can create a sense of mutual understanding and empathy.

   - Use "I" statements to express your feelings and encourage others to do the same.

8. **Learn About Different Perspectives**: Educate yourself about different cultures, backgrounds, and experiences. Exposure to diverse perspectives enhances your ability to empathize with others.

   - Read books, watch documentaries, and engage in conversations that broaden your understanding of different experiences.

9. **Practise Mindfulness**: Mindfulness helps you stay present and attuned to others' emotions. Practising mindfulness enhances your ability to respond empathetically.

   - Engage in mindfulness exercises, such as meditation and deep breathing, to improve your awareness and presence.

10. **Reflect on Empathetic Interactions**: Reflect on your interactions and consider how you can improve your empathy. Regular reflection helps you identify areas for growth and strengthen your empathetic skills.

    - Keep a journal to document your reflections and track your progress in cultivating empathy.

Conclusion

Cultivating empathy is essential for strengthening relationships and building a compassionate community. Here are key strategies to develop a deeper understanding and connection with others:

- Practise active listening
- Ask open-ended questions
- Validate feelings
- Practise perspective-taking
- Show compassion
- Be present
- Share your own feelings
- Learn about different perspectives
- Practise mindfulness

- Reflect on empathetic interactions

As Atticus Finch from "To Kill a Mockingbird" said***, "You never really understand a person until you consider things from his point of view."*** Embrace empathy, and you will create stronger, more supportive relationships and communities.

Live Authentically: The Path to Genuine Happiness and Success

Living authentically means being true to oneself and aligning one's actions with one's personal values. This approach fosters genuine happiness and success by creating a life that is fulfilling and true to who one is. As Oscar Wilde famously said*, "Be yourself; everyone else is already taken."* Embracing authenticity allows you to live with integrity and find deeper satisfaction in personal and professional endeavours.

The Importance of Living Authentically

1. **Increased Happiness**: Authenticity leads to greater life satisfaction and happiness by allowing you to live in harmony with your true self.
2. **Stronger Relationships**: Being genuine fosters trust and deeper connections with others, as people appreciate and are drawn to authenticity.
3. **Enhanced Confidence**: Living according to your values boosts self-esteem and confidence, as you are not trying to be someone you're not.
4. **Reduced Stress**: Authentic living reduces the stress and anxiety that comes from trying to meet others' expectations or living a life that doesn't feel right.
5. **Greater Success**: Aligning your actions with your true self often leads to greater professional and personal success, as you are more motivated and passionate about your pursuits.

Strategies to Live Authentically

1. **Know Yourself**: Spend time reflecting on your values, passions, and beliefs. Understanding who you are and what matters to you is the foundation of authentic living.

   - Journaling, meditation, and introspective practise can help you gain clarity about your true self.

2. **Align Actions with Values**: Ensure that your actions and decisions reflect your personal values and beliefs. Consistency between your values and actions is key to authenticity.

   - Regularly review your goals and actions to ensure they align with your core values.

3. **Embrace Vulnerability**: Be open and honest about your thoughts, feelings, and experiences. Embracing vulnerability strengthens your authenticity and deepens connections with others.

   - Share your true self with others, even if it sometimes feels uncomfortable.

4. **Set Boundaries**: Establish boundaries that protect your time, energy, and well-being. Respecting your limits is an essential aspect of living authentically.

   - Communicate your boundaries clearly and assertively to others.

5. **Say No When Necessary**: Learn to say no to commitments and requests that do not align with your

values or priorities. Saying no is a powerful way to stay true to yourself.

- Practise saying no with confidence and without guilt.

6. **Pursue Your Passions**: Engage in activities and pursuits that ignite your passion and bring you joy. Following your passions is a key component of authentic living.

- Make time for hobbies, interests, and projects that you are passionate about.

7. **Practise Self-Compassion**: Be kind to yourself and practise self-compassion, especially during challenging times. Self-compassion reinforces your authenticity by allowing you to accept yourself fully.

- Treat yourself with the kindness and understanding you would offer a friend.

8. **Surround Yourself with Supportive People**: Build a network of friends, family, and colleagues who support and encourage your authentic self. Positive relationships reinforce your commitment to authenticity.

- Seek out relationships that uplift and inspire you to be your true self.

9. **Live in the Present**: Focus on the present moment and engage fully in your experiences. Mindfulness helps you stay connected to your true self and live authentically.

- Practise mindfulness techniques, such as meditation and deep breathing, to stay present.

10. **Reflect and Adjust**: Regularly reflect on your life and make adjustments as needed to stay true to your authentic self. Self-reflection helps you stay aligned with your values and goals.

- Set aside time for regular self-reflection to evaluate your actions and choices.

Conclusion

Living authentically is the path to genuine happiness and success. Here are key strategies to help you live a life true to who you are:

- Know yourself
- Align your actions with your values
- Embrace vulnerability
- Set boundaries
- Say no when necessary
- Pursue your passions
- Practise self-compassion
- Surround yourself with supportive people
- Live in the present
- Regularly reflect and adjust

As Brené Brown wisely said, ***"Authenticity is the daily practice of letting go of who we think we're supposed to be and embracing who we are."*** Embrace authenticity, and you will find greater joy, fulfilment, and success in all areas of your life.

Set Clear Goals: Defining Your Path to Success

Setting clear goals—both short-term and long-term—is essential for maintaining focus and direction in your career. Knowing what you want to achieve provides a roadmap for your professional journey, helping you stay motivated and on track. As the motivational speaker Zig Ziglar once said, ***"A goal properly set is halfway reached."*** By defining your career goals, you set the foundation for achieving your aspirations and reaching your full potential.

The Importance of Setting Clear Goals

1. **Enhanced Focus**: Clear goals provide a sense of direction, helping you prioritise tasks and activities that align with your objectives.
2. **Increased Motivation**: Well-defined goals motivate you by giving you something to strive towards and look forward to.
3. **Improved Decision-Making**: Goals are a benchmark for making decisions, ensuring that your choices support your long-term vision.
4. **Greater Accountability**: Setting goals holds you accountable for your progress and encourages you to take responsibility for your actions.
5. **Measure of Progress**: Goals provide a way to measure progress and celebrate achievements.

Strategies to Set Clear Goals

1. **Define Your Vision**: Start by envisioning where you want to be in the future. Think about your long-term aspirations and what success looks like to you.

   - Reflect on your passions, strengths, and values to identify your ultimate career goals.

2. **Break Down Goals**: Divide your long-term goals into smaller, manageable short-term goals. This makes the larger objectives more attainable and less overwhelming.

   - Set goals for different time frames, such as daily, weekly, monthly, and yearly targets.

3. **Use SMART Criteria**: Ensure your goals are Specific, Measurable, Achievable, Relevant, and Time-bound. The SMART framework provides clarity and structure, making your goals more effective.

   - Specific: Clearly define what you want to achieve.
   - Measurable: Determine how you will track progress.
   - Achievable: Set realistic goals that are within your reach.
   - Relevant: Ensure your goals align with your broader objectives.
   - Time-bound: Establish a deadline for achieving your goals.

4. **Write Down Your Goals**: Documenting your goals reinforces your commitment and provides a reference point to review regularly.

- Keep a goal journal or use digital tools to track your goals and progress.

5. **Create an Action Plan**: Develop a detailed action plan outlining the steps needed to achieve your goals. An action plan provides a clear path forward and helps you stay organised.

   - Break down each goal into actionable tasks and assign deadlines to keep yourself on track.

6. **Stay Flexible**: Be prepared to adjust your goals and action plans as needed. Flexibility allows you to adapt to changing circumstances and align with your evolving vision.

   - Regularly review and update your goals to reflect new insights and opportunities.

7. **Seek Support and Feedback**: Share your goals with mentors, colleagues, or friends who can provide support, encouragement, and constructive feedback.

   - Regular check-ins with a mentor or accountability partner can help you stay focused and motivated.

8. **Celebrate Milestones**: Acknowledge and celebrate your achievements, no matter how small. Celebrating milestones boosts motivation and reinforces your commitment to your goals.

   - Reward yourself for reaching significant milestones to maintain enthusiasm and momentum.

9. **Reflect and Learn**: Periodically reflect on your progress and experiences. Reflecting on what worked and what didn't help you learn and improve your goal-setting process.

   - Use reflection to identify areas for growth and adjust your goals accordingly.

10. **Stay Committed**: Stay focused and persistent to maintain a strong commitment to your goals. Overcoming obstacles and staying dedicated to your vision lead to long-term success.

    - Remind yourself regularly of the reasons behind your goals and the benefits of achieving them.

Conclusion

Setting clear goals is crucial for defining your path to success. Here are key strategies to help you achieve your career aspirations:

- Define your vision
- Break down goals
- Use the SMART criteria
- Write down your goals
- Create an action plan
- Stay flexible
- Seek support and feedback
- Celebrate milestones
- Reflect and learn
- Stay committed

As Henry David Thoreau wisely said**, *"Go confidently in the direction of your dreams. Live the life you have imagined."*** Embrace the power of goal-setting, and you will create a focused, motivated, and successful career journey.

Seek Mentorship: The Power of Guidance, Feedback, and Support

Finding a mentor within your organisation or industry can be a game-changer for your career. A mentor provides valuable guidance, feedback, and support, helping you navigate challenges and achieve your professional goals. As Oprah Winfrey once said, "A mentor is someone who allows you to see the hope inside yourself." Embracing mentorship can unlock your potential and propel you toward success.

The Importance of Seeking Mentorship

1. **Guidance and Advice**: Mentors offer valuable insights and advice based on their experience, helping you make informed decisions.
2. **Career Development**: A mentor can help identify growth opportunities, develop new skills, and advance your career.
3. **Networking**: Mentors can introduce you to their network, providing access to valuable connections and opportunities.
4. **Feedback and Improvement**: Constructive feedback from a mentor helps you improve your performance and develop professionally.
5. **Support and Encouragement**: A mentor provides emotional support and encouragement, boosting your confidence and resilience.

Strategies to Seek and Build a Mentorship Relationship

1. **Identify Potential Mentors**: Look for potential mentors within your organisation or industry with experience and expertise. Consider their career achievements, values, and willingness to mentor.

   - Attend industry events, join professional groups, and network to identify potential mentors.

2. **Clarify Your Goals**: Before approaching a mentor, clarify your goals and what you hope to gain from the mentorship. Understanding your objectives will help you find a mentor who aligns with your needs.

   - Reflect on your career aspirations, challenges, and areas for improvement.

3. **Reach Out Professionally**: Approach potential mentors professionally and respectfully. Express your admiration for their work and explain why you seek their guidance.

   - Send a thoughtful email or request a meeting to discuss the possibility of mentorship.

4. **Be Specific**: Clearly articulate what you want in a mentor and how you believe they can help you. Specificity demonstrates your seriousness and commitment.

   - Outline your goals, the type of guidance you seek, and the areas where you need support.

5. **Build a Relationship**: Focus on building a genuine relationship with your mentor. Show interest in their

experiences and insights, and be open and honest in your interactions.

- Regularly communicate and engage with your mentor, showing appreciation for their time and support.

6. **Be Open to Feedback**: Embrace constructive feedback from your mentor and use it to improve your skills and performance. Openness to feedback is crucial for growth.

- Act on the feedback provided and demonstrate your willingness to learn and develop.

7. **Show Initiative**: Take the initiative in your mentorship relationship by setting up meetings, preparing questions, and actively seeking advice. Your proactive approach shows your dedication.

- Schedule regular check-ins and come prepared with specific topics or questions to discuss.

8. **Respect Their Time**: Be mindful of your mentor's time and commitments. Respect their availability and be punctual and prepared for meetings.

- Keep meetings concise and focused, and always thank them for their time and insights.

9. **Be Grateful and Give Back**: Express gratitude for your mentor's guidance and support. Consider ways you can give back, whether by sharing your progress or offering assistance in return.

- Acknowledge their impact on your development and look for opportunities to support them or pay it forward to others.

10. **Reflect and Adjust**: Regularly reflect on your mentorship experience and adjust your approach as needed. Continuous reflection helps you maximise the benefits of the relationship.

- Assess your progress and seek feedback from your mentor on how to improve the mentorship dynamic.

Conclusion

Seeking mentorship is a powerful strategy for gaining career guidance, feedback, and support. Here are key strategies to develop a meaningful and impactful mentorship relationship:

- Identify potential mentors
- Clarify your goals
- Reach out professionally
- Be specific
- Build a relationship
- Be open to feedback
- Show initiative
- Respect their time
- Be grateful
- Reflect and adjust

As John C. Maxwell wisely said, ***"One of the greatest values of mentors is the ability to see ahead what others cannot see and to help them navigate a course to their***

destination. " Embrace the power of mentorship, and you will find greater success, growth, and fulfilment in your professional journey.

Embrace Continuous Learning: The Key to Professional Growth and Success

Staying curious and continuously seeking opportunities to learn new skills and knowledge is essential for professional growth and success. Embracing continuous learning keeps you adaptable, relevant, and competitive in an ever-evolving job market. *As Albert Einstein once said, "Once you stop learning, you start dying."* By prioritising lifelong learning, you ensure your personal and professional development never stagnates.

The Importance of Continuous Learning

1. **Adaptability**: Continuous learning helps you adapt to changes in your industry and keeps your skills relevant.
2. **Career Advancement**: Acquiring new skills and knowledge opens doors to new opportunities and career growth.
3. **Increased Innovation**: Learning fosters creativity and innovation, allowing you to contribute fresh ideas and solutions.
4. **Enhanced Confidence**: Expanding your skill set boosts your confidence and self-efficacy in your professional capabilities.
5. **Personal Fulfilment**: Pursuing knowledge enriches your personal life and contributes to overall satisfaction and fulfilment.

Strategies to Embrace Continuous Learning

1. **Set Learning Goals**: Identify specific skills and knowledge areas you want to develop. Setting clear learning goals provides direction and motivation for your learning journey.

   - Use the SMART criteria (Specific, Measurable, Achievable, Relevant, Time-bound) to set effective learning goals.

2. **Take Online Courses**: Enrol in online courses and certifications relevant to your field. Many platforms offer flexible and affordable learning options.

   - Websites like Coursera, Udemy, and LinkedIn Learning offer courses on a wide range of topics.

3. **Read Regularly**: Develop a habit of reading books, articles, and journals related to your industry. Reading broadens your knowledge and keeps you updated on trends and developments.

   - Create a reading list and set aside time each day or week for reading.

4. **Attend Workshops and Seminars**: Participate in workshops, seminars, and conferences to gain new insights and network with industry professionals.

   - Look for local and virtual events that align with your learning goals.

5. **Seek Mentorship**: Find mentors who can share their expertise and provide guidance on your learning

journey. Mentors can offer valuable insights and help you navigate your career path.

- Engage in regular discussions with your mentors to learn from their experiences.

6. **Join Professional Associations**: Become a member of professional associations and organisations related to your field. These groups often provide resources, training, and networking opportunities.

- Participate actively in association events and utilise available resources.

7. **Engage in Hands-On Projects**: Apply your learning by working on hands-on projects and real-world tasks. Practical experience reinforces theoretical knowledge and builds practical skills.

- Look for volunteer opportunities, internships, or side projects to gain practical experience.

8. **Stay Curious**: Cultivate a curious mindset and ask questions. Curiosity drives the desire to learn and discover new things.

- Approach every situation with a willingness to learn and explore new possibilities.

9. **Utilise Technology**: Leverage technology to access a wealth of learning resources, from educational apps to online forums and podcasts.

- Explore apps like Duolingo for language learning or Khan Academy for diverse subjects.

10. **Reflect and Review**: Regularly reflect on your learning progress and review what you've learned. Reflection helps consolidate knowledge and identify areas for further growth.

- Keep a learning journal to document your progress, insights, and future learning goals.

Conclusion

Embracing continuous learning is crucial for professional growth and success. Here are key strategies to cultivate a lifelong learning habit:

- Set learning goals
- Take online courses
- Read regularly
- Attend workshops and seminars
- Seek mentorship
- Join professional associations
- Engage in hands-on projects
- Stay curious
- Utilise technology
- Reflect and review

As Mahatma Gandhi wisely said, ***"Live as if you were to die tomorrow. Learn as if you were to live forever."*** Prioritise continuous learning, and you will unlock endless opportunities for growth, innovation, and fulfilment in your career.

Show Initiative: The Power of Proactive Attitude

Demonstrating initiative by taking on additional responsibilities and suggesting improvements is a key factor in career advancement and personal growth. A proactive attitude showcases your commitment and drive and positions you as a valuable and innovative team member. As former U.S. President John Quincy Adams once said, "If your actions inspire others to dream more, learn more, do more, and become more, you are a leader." Embracing initiative can transform your career and open doors to new opportunities.

The Importance of Showing Initiative

1. **Career Advancement**: Taking initiative sets you apart as a proactive and motivated employee, which can lead to promotions and new opportunities.
2. **Skill Development**: Engaging in additional responsibilities helps you develop new skills and gain valuable experience.
3. **Increased Visibility**: Proactively suggesting improvements and taking on tasks increases your visibility within the organisation.
4. **Enhanced Problem-Solving**: Initiative often involves identifying and addressing challenges and enhancing problem-solving abilities.

5. **Stronger Leadership**: Demonstrating initiative is a key trait of effective leaders, fostering trust and respect among colleagues.

Strategies to Show Initiative

1. **Identify Opportunities for Improvement**: Observe your work environment and processes to identify areas that could benefit from enhancement. Suggest practical solutions to improve efficiency or quality.

    - Keep a list of potential improvements and prioritise those that align with your skills and the organisation's goals.

2. **Volunteer for Additional Responsibilities**: Take on tasks or projects outside your regular duties to demonstrate your willingness to contribute and learn.

    - Look for opportunities to assist colleagues, lead projects, or take on roles that align with your career goals.

3. **Develop New Skills**: Proactively seek out learning opportunities to develop new skills that can benefit your role and the organisation.

    - Enrol in relevant courses, attend workshops or seek mentorship to enhance your capabilities.

4. **Communicate Proactively**: Keep your supervisors and colleagues informed about your progress and any initiatives you are undertaking. Open communication fosters collaboration and support.

- Regularly update your team on the status of projects and share your ideas for improvements.

5. **Take Ownership of Projects**: Show responsibility by taking ownership of projects from start to finish. Demonstrate your commitment by delivering high-quality work and meeting deadlines.

   - Create detailed plans and set milestones to ensure successful project completion.

6. **Be a Problem Solver**: When challenges arise, approach them with a solution-oriented mindset. Present well-thought-out solutions rather than just highlighting the problems.

   - Analyze the issue, brainstorm possible solutions, and propose actionable steps to resolve it.

7. **Show Enthusiasm and Positivity**: Maintain a positive attitude and show enthusiasm for your work. Positivity and enthusiasm are contagious and can inspire others.

   - Encourage and motivate your colleagues, creating a supportive and productive work environment.

8. **Seek Feedback and Act on It**: Regularly seek feedback from supervisors and peers to improve your performance. Use this feedback to refine your approach and enhance your contributions.

   - Actively listen to feedback, thank those who provide it, and implement the suggestions for improvement.

9. **Network Within Your Organisation**: Build relationships with colleagues across different departments. Networking enhances collaboration and increases your visibility within the organisation.

   - Attend company events, join committees, and engage in cross-departmental projects.

10. **Reflect and Learn from Experience**: Reflect on your experiences and learn from both successes and setbacks. Continuous reflection helps you identify areas for growth and improvement.

    - Keep a journal to document your initiatives, what worked well, and what could be improved.

Conclusion

Showing initiative by taking on additional responsibilities and suggesting improvements is crucial for career advancement and personal growth. Here are key strategies to demonstrate a proactive attitude:

- Identify opportunities for improvement
- Volunteer for additional responsibilities
- Develop new skills
- Communicate proactively
- Take ownership of projects
- Be a problem solver
- Show enthusiasm and positivity
- Seek feedback
- Network within your organisation
- Reflect on your experiences

As Tony Robbins famously said, ***"The path to success is to take massive, determined action."*** Embrace initiative and position yourself for greater success and fulfilment in your professional journey.

Be Punctual and Reliable: Building Trust Through Consistency

Being punctual and reliable is fundamental to building trust with colleagues and superiors. Consistently being on time for work, meetings, and deadlines demonstrates your commitment, professionalism, and respect for others' time. As the famous saying goes, "Time is money." By valuing punctuality and reliability, you enhance your reputation and contribute to a productive and harmonious work environment.

The Importance of Punctuality and Reliability

1. **Builds Trust**: Consistently meeting commitments fosters trust and confidence among colleagues and superiors.
2. **Enhances Professionalism**: Punctuality and reliability are key indicators of professionalism and work ethic.
3. **Improves Efficiency**: Being on time and dependable ensures that projects and tasks are completed efficiently and on schedule.
4. **Strengthens Relationships**: Reliable behaviour builds strong, respectful relationships with your team and supervisors.
5. **Reduces Stress**: Consistency and punctuality reduce last-minute stress and create a more organised work environment.

Strategies to Be Punctual and Reliable

1. **Plan Ahead**: Anticipate potential obstacles and plan your schedule accordingly. Allow extra time for unforeseen delays to ensure punctuality.
   - Use calendars, planners, or scheduling apps to organise your time and set reminders for important commitments.
2. **Set Priorities**: Identify your most important tasks and focus on completing them first. Prioritising helps you meet deadlines and manage your time effectively.
   - Create a daily to-do list, ranking tasks by urgency and importance.
3. **Establish Routines**: Develop consistent routines that support punctuality and reliability. Regular habits make it easier to manage your time and stay organised.
   - Set a regular bedtime and wake-up time to ensure you start your day on schedule.
4. **Communicate Clearly**: Keep your colleagues and supervisors informed about your progress and any potential delays. Clear communication helps manage expectations and demonstrates accountability.
   - Notify relevant parties as soon as possible if you anticipate being late or missing a deadline.
5. **Use Time Management Tools**: Leverage time management tools and techniques to stay on track. Techniques such as the Pomodoro Technique or time blocking can enhance productivity and punctuality.
   - Experiment with different time management methods to find what works best for you.

6. **Prepare in Advance**: Prepare for meetings and deadlines in advance to avoid last-minute rushes. Preparation ensures that you can deliver high-quality work on time.

   - Gather necessary materials, review agendas, and complete preliminary tasks beforehand.

7. **Hold Yourself Accountable**: Take personal responsibility for meeting your commitments. Accountability reinforces your reliability and professionalism.

   - Set deadlines earlier than the actual deadlines to give yourself a buffer.

8. **Monitor Your Progress**: Regularly check your progress on tasks and projects. Monitoring helps you stay on track and adjust as needed to meet deadlines.

   - Use project management tools or tracking sheets to monitor your progress.

9. **Seek Feedback**: Ask colleagues and supervisors about your punctuality and reliability. Constructive feedback can help you identify areas for improvement.

   - Act on the feedback provided and continuously enhance your reliability.

10. **Reflect and Improve**: Reflect on your experiences and identify what worked well and could be improved. Continuous reflection helps you refine your time management skills.

    - Keep a journal to document your reflections and set goals for improvement.

Conclusion

Being punctual and reliable is essential for building trust and maintaining professionalism in the workplace. Here are key strategies to help you consistently meet your commitments and build a strong reputation:

Plan ahead

Set priorities

Establish routines

Communicate clearly

Use time management tools

Prepare in advance

Hold yourself accountable

Monitor your progress

Seek feedback

Reflect and improve

As Benjamin Franklin wisely said, ***"By failing to prepare, you are preparing to fail."*** Embrace punctuality and reliability, and you will foster trust, efficiency, and success in your professional life.

Focus on Personal Branding: Building a Professional Image Online and Offline

Building a strong personal brand is essential for career success in today's digital and interconnected world. Your personal brand reflects your professional aspirations, values, and expertise online and offline. As Jeff Bezos, the founder of Amazon, famously said, "Your brand is what other people say about you when you're not in the room." By focusing on personal branding, you can enhance your professional image and open doors to new opportunities.

The Importance of Personal Branding

1. **Enhanced Professional Image**: A strong personal brand establishes you as a credible and authoritative figure in your field.
2. **Increased Opportunities**: Effective personal branding attracts new career opportunities, networking connections, and potential collaborations.
3. **Clear Communication of Values**: Your brand communicates your professional values, goals, and strengths, helping others understand what you stand for.
4. **Greater Visibility**: A well-managed personal brand increases your online and offline visibility and presence.
5. **Career Advancement**: A strong personal brand can lead to promotions, job offers, and other career advancements.

Strategies to Build Your Personal Brand

1. **Define Your Brand**: Identify your unique strengths, skills, values, and professional goals. Understanding what sets you apart is the foundation of your personal brand.

   - Reflect on your career aspirations, core values, and key strengths to define your personal brand statement.

2. **Develop a Professional Online Presence**: Ensure your social media profiles, such as LinkedIn, Twitter, and professional websites, reflect your personal brand. Consistency across platforms is crucial.

   - Optimise your LinkedIn profile with a professional photo, a compelling headline, and a detailed summary of your experiences and skills.

3. **Create Valuable Content**: Share content that showcases your expertise and adds value to your audience. This could include blog posts, articles, videos, or social media updates.

   - Regularly publish content related to your industry, and engage with others by commenting on and sharing their posts.

4. **Network Actively**: Build and maintain relationships with professionals in your field. Networking enhances your visibility and provides opportunities for collaboration and growth.

- Attend industry events, join professional associations, and participate in online forums and groups.

5. **Seek Endorsements and Recommendations**: Collect endorsements and recommendations from colleagues, mentors, and clients. Positive testimonials reinforce your credibility and expertise.

   - Request recommendations on LinkedIn and display testimonials on your professional website or portfolio.

6. **Stay Authentic**: Authenticity is key to a strong personal brand. Be genuine in your interactions and stay true to your values and beliefs.

   - Share personal stories and experiences that highlight your journey and growth, making your brand relatable and trustworthy.

7. **Monitor Your Online Presence**: Regularly check your online presence to ensure it aligns with your personal brand. Address any inconsistencies or negative content promptly.

   - Use tools like Google Alerts to monitor mentions of your name and stay informed about your online reputation.

8. **Continuously Improve and Update**: Personal branding is an ongoing process. Continuously improve your skills, update your profiles, and adapt to changes in your industry.

- Take courses, attend workshops, and stay updated on industry trends to keep your brand relevant and competitive.

9. **Engage with Your Audience**: Actively engage with your audience by responding to comments, participating in discussions, and building relationships.

   - Show appreciation for your audience's support and encourage interaction and feedback.

10. **Maintain a Professional Offline Presence**: Your offline presence should reflect your personal brand just as much as your online presence. Professionalism, attire, and behaviour matter.

    - Attend events and meetings prepared, dress appropriately, and conduct yourself with integrity and professionalism.

Conclusion

Focusing on personal branding is crucial for building a professional image and achieving career success. Here are key strategies to effectively manage your personal brand:

- Define your brand
- Develop a professional online presence
- Create valuable content
- Network actively
- Seek endorsements
- Stay authentic
- Monitor your online presence
- Continuously improve

- Engage with your audience
- Maintain a professional offline presence

As Tom Peters, a business management writer, said, **"We are CEOs of our own companies: Me Inc. To be in business today, our most important job is to be head marketer for the brand called You."** Embrace personal branding, and you will enhance your professional image and open doors to new opportunities and career growth.

Seek Feedback and Act on It: The Key to Continuous Improvement

Regularly seeking feedback from supervisors and peers and using it constructively is essential for personal and professional growth. Feedback provides valuable insights into your strengths and areas for improvement, helping you enhance your performance and achieve your goals. As Bill Gates once said, "We all need people who will give us feedback. That's how we improve." Embracing feedback as a tool for development can lead to significant progress in your career.

The Importance of Seeking Feedback

1. **Identifies Strengths and Weaknesses**: Feedback helps you understand what you're doing well and where you can improve, providing a balanced view of your performance.
2. **Enhances Skills and Competencies**: Constructive feedback guides you on developing and refining your skills, leading to continuous improvement.
3. **Boosts Performance**: Acting on feedback leads to better performance, increased productivity, and higher quality work.
4. **Builds Trust and Relationships**: Regularly seeking feedback shows that you value others' opinions and are committed to growth, fostering trust and stronger relationships.

5. **Encourages Open Communication**: A feedback-oriented approach promotes a culture of open communication and continuous learning within teams and organisations.

Strategies to Seek and Use Feedback Effectively

1. **Ask Specific Questions**: When seeking feedback, ask specific questions to get detailed and actionable insights. General questions often lead to vague responses.

   - For example, ask, "How can I improve my presentation skills?" instead of "How did I do?"

2. **Choose the Right Time and Place**: Request feedback at an appropriate time and place to ensure thoughtful and constructive responses. Avoid asking for feedback in rushed or informal settings.

   - Schedule one-on-one meetings or feedback sessions to have focused discussions.

3. **Be Open and Receptive**: Approach feedback with an open mind and a willingness to learn. Avoid becoming defensive or dismissive when receiving constructive criticism.

   - Listen actively, take notes, and ask clarifying questions to understand the feedback fully.

4. **Actively Seek Feedback**: Don't wait for feedback to come to you; proactively seek it from various sources, including supervisors, peers, and subordinates.

- Regularly ask for feedback during performance reviews, team meetings, and informal check-ins.

5. **Reflect on Feedback**: Take time to reflect on the feedback you receive and identify key takeaways. Consider how the feedback aligns with your goals and areas for improvement.

   - Write down the feedback and reflect on its implications for your development.

6. **Create an Action Plan**: Develop a clear action plan based on the feedback to address areas for improvement. Set specific, measurable goals to track your progress.

   - Outline the steps you will take to implement the feedback and achieve your goals. For example, if the feedback highlights a need to improve your communication skills, your action plan might include attending workshops, reading relevant books, and practising with a mentor.

7. **Implement Changes**: Implement your action plan and make the necessary changes to improve your performance. Demonstrating that you can act on feedback shows your commitment to growth.

   - Consistently work on the areas identified in the feedback and monitor your progress.

8. **Seek Regular Check-Ins**: Arrange follow-up meetings with your feedback providers to discuss your progress

and get additional input. Regular check-ins help keep you on track and show your dedication to improvement.

- Use these sessions to review your action plan, discuss challenges, and adjust your approach.

9. **Show Appreciation**: Thank those who provide you with feedback. Expressing gratitude reinforces positive relationships and encourages others to continue offering valuable insights.

- A simple thank-you note or verbal acknowledgement can go a long way in showing appreciation.

10. **Embrace a Growth Mindset**: Adopt a growth mindset, believing your abilities can develop through effort and learning. A growth mindset makes you more receptive to feedback and committed to continuous improvement.

- Focus on progress rather than perfection and view challenges as growth opportunities.

Conclusion

Seeking and acting on feedback is a powerful strategy for continuous improvement and professional development. Here are key strategies to leverage feedback to enhance your performance:

- Ask specific questions
- Choose the right time and place
- Be open and receptive

- Actively seek feedback
- Reflect on it
- Create an action plan
- Implement changes
- Seek regular check-ins
- Show appreciation
- Embrace a growth mindset

As Ken Blanchard, a renowned management expert, said**,** ***"Feedback is the breakfast of champions."*** Make feedback a regular part of your professional journey, and you will achieve greater success and fulfilment in your career.

Maintain a Positive Attitude: The Power of Optimism and Resilience

Staying optimistic and resilient is crucial for personal and professional success, even when facing challenges. A positive attitude helps you navigate difficulties gracefully and inspires and motivates those around you. Winston Churchill once said, ***"A pessimist sees the difficulty in every opportunity; an optimist sees the opportunity in every difficulty."*** Embracing a positive attitude can transform your work environment and drive success for you and your team.

The Importance of Maintaining a Positive Attitude

1. **Increased Resilience**: A positive attitude helps you bounce back from setbacks and maintain focus on your goals.
2. **Enhanced Productivity**: Optimism boosts motivation and energy, increasing productivity and efficiency.
3. **Improved Relationships**: Positivity fosters better colleague relationships, creating a supportive and collaborative work environment.
4. **Health Benefits**: A positive mindset is linked to better physical and mental health, reduced stress, and improved overall well-being.
5. **Inspirational Leadership**: Leaders with a positive attitude inspire and motivate their teams, fostering a culture of optimism and perseverance.

Strategies to Maintain a Positive Attitude

1. **Practise Gratitude**: Regularly acknowledge and appreciate the positive aspects of your life and work. Gratitude shifts your focus from challenges to opportunities.

   - Keep a gratitude journal and write down three things you're grateful for each day.

2. **Surround Yourself with Positivity**: Build a network of supportive and positive individuals who uplift and encourage you.

   - Engage with colleagues and friends who maintain a positive outlook and avoid negative influences.

3. **Focus on Solutions**: When faced with challenges, focus on finding solutions rather than dwelling on problems. A solution-oriented mindset fosters positivity and resilience.

   - Brainstorm possible solutions and take proactive steps to address challenges.

4. **Take Care of Your Health**: Prioritise physical and mental well-being through regular exercise, a balanced diet, and adequate sleep. Good health supports a positive mindset.

   - Incorporate physical activities into your routine and practise mindfulness or meditation to reduce stress.

5. **Set Realistic Goals**: Establish achievable goals and celebrate your progress. Realistic goals provide a sense of accomplishment and motivation.

   - Break larger goals into smaller, manageable tasks and track your progress.

6. **Practise Positive Self-Talk**: Replace negative thoughts with positive affirmations. Positive self-talk reinforces confidence and optimism.

   - Use affirmations like "I can handle this challenge" or "I am capable and resilient."

7. **Learn from Setbacks**: View setbacks as learning opportunities rather than failures. Reflect on what you can learn from the experience and how you can grow.

   - Analyze setbacks objectively and identify steps to improve and move forward.

8. **Celebrate Successes**: Acknowledge and celebrate your achievements, no matter how small. Celebrating successes boosts morale and reinforces a positive attitude.

   - Share your successes with your team and appreciate your hard work.

9. **Stay Flexible and Adaptable**: Embrace change and adapt to new circumstances. Flexibility helps you maintain a positive outlook in the face of uncertainty.

   - Approach changes with an open mind and a willingness to learn and grow.

10. **Help Others**: Supporting and encouraging others fosters a positive environment and enhances your own sense of well-being.

- Offer assistance, provide positive feedback, and celebrate others' achievements.

Conclusion

Maintaining a positive attitude is essential for navigating challenges and achieving success. Here are key strategies to cultivate a positive mindset:

- Practise gratitude
- Surround yourself with positivity
- Focus on solutions
- Take care of your health
- Set realistic goals
- Practise positive self-talk
- Learn from setbacks
- Celebrate successes
- Stay flexible and adaptable
- Help others

As Charles R. Swindoll said, ***"Life is 10% what happens to us and 90% how we react to it."*** Embrace a positive attitude, and you will inspire your team, enhance your well-being, and drive personal and professional success.

Work on Emotional Intelligence: The Key to Effective Leadership and Teamwork

Developing emotional intelligence (EI) is crucial for effective leadership and teamwork. Emotional intelligence involves understanding and managing your own emotions, as well as recognising and influencing the emotions of others. As Daniel Goleman, a pioneer in EI, stated, "Emotional intelligence is the sine qua non of leadership." Enhancing your emotional intelligence can improve your leadership capabilities, foster better relationships, and create a positive and productive work environment.

The Importance of Emotional Intelligence

1. **Enhanced Leadership**: Leaders with high EI can inspire, motivate, and connect with their team members, leading to better performance and engagement.
2. **Improved Teamwork**: Emotional intelligence fosters a collaborative and supportive team environment, improving communication and cooperation.
3. **Better Decision-Making**: EI allows you to manage stress and emotions, leading to more rational and effective decision-making.
4. **Increased Self-Awareness**: Understanding your emotions helps you recognise your strengths and weaknesses, leading to personal growth and improved performance.

5. **Stronger Relationships**: EI enhances empathy and social skills, leading to more meaningful and positive relationships with colleagues and clients.

Strategies to Develop Emotional Intelligence

1. **Develop Self-Awareness**: Understand your emotions, strengths, and weaknesses. Self-awareness is the foundation of emotional intelligence.

   - Reflect on your emotional responses and identify patterns. Keep a journal to track your feelings and reactions.

2. **Practise Self-Regulation**: Learn to manage your emotions and stay in control, especially in stressful situations. Self-regulation involves thinking before acting.

   - Practise deep breathing, mindfulness, or meditation to help manage stress and maintain composure.

3. **Enhance Empathy**: Understand and share the feelings of others. Empathy allows you to connect with others more deeply and respond appropriately to their emotions.

   - Actively listen to others, validate their feelings, and try to see situations from their perspective.

4. **Improve Social Skills**: Develop strong communication and interpersonal skills. Social skills are essential for building and maintaining positive relationships.

- Engage in active listening, provide constructive feedback, and improve your verbal and non-verbal communication skills.

5. **Cultivate Motivation**: Stay motivated and committed to your goals. Intrinsic motivation drives you to achieve your best and inspires those around you.

   - Set personal and professional goals that align with your values and passions.

6. **Seek Feedback**: Ask for feedback from colleagues and mentors to gain insights into your emotional intelligence. Use this feedback to identify areas for improvement.

   - Regularly seek feedback and be open to constructive criticism.

7. **Practise Mindfulness**: Mindfulness helps you stay present and aware of your emotions and the emotions of others. It enhances your ability to respond rather than react.

   - Incorporate mindfulness practices into your daily routine, such as meditation or breathing.

8. **Develop Conflict Resolution Skills**: Learn to handle conflicts constructively and calmly. Effective conflict resolution is a key component of emotional intelligence.

   - Approach conflicts with a solution-oriented mindset and seek to understand all perspectives.

9. **Build Resilience**: Strengthen your ability to bounce back from setbacks and challenges. Resilience is essential for maintaining emotional balance.

   - Practise self-care, maintain a positive outlook, and develop coping strategies for stress.

10. **Engage in Continuous Learning**: Emotional intelligence is a lifelong journey. Continuously seek opportunities to learn and grow in your EI skills.

    - Attend workshops, read books on emotional intelligence, and engage in self-reflection and self-improvement activities.

Conclusion

Working on emotional intelligence is key to effective leadership and teamwork. Here are key strategies to enhance your EI and create a positive impact in your personal and professional life:

- Develop self-awareness
- Practise self-regulation
- Enhance empathy
- Improve social skills
- Cultivate motivation
- Seek feedback
- Practise mindfulness
- Develop conflict resolution skills
- Build resilience
- Engage in continuous learning

As Maya Angelou wisely said, **"People will forget what you said, people will forget what you did, but people will never forget how you made them feel."** Embrace emotional intelligence, and you will foster stronger relationships, inspire others, and achieve greater success in all areas of your life.

As Maya Angelou wisely said, **"People will forget what you said, people will forget what you did, but people will never forget how you made them feel."** Embrace emotional intelligence, and you will foster stronger relationships, inspire others, and achieve greater success in all areas of your life.

Balance Work and Life: Setting Boundaries for a Healthier and More Productive Life

Achieving a healthy work-life balance is essential for overall well-being and productivity. Setting boundaries between work and personal life helps prevent burnout and ensures you can enjoy both aspects of your life fully. As the motivational speaker Zig Ziglar once said, "Work is something you do, not something you are." Embracing this philosophy can lead to a more fulfilling and productive life.

The Importance of Work-Life Balance

1. **Prevents Burnout**: Overworking can lead to physical and mental exhaustion. A balanced approach ensures you remain energised and motivated.
2. **Increases Productivity**: Taking breaks and having downtime can boost your productivity and creativity at work.
3. **Enhances Relationships**: Balancing work and personal life allow you to spend quality time with family and friends, strengthening relationships.
4. **Improves Health**: A balanced lifestyle promotes better physical and mental health, reduces stress, and increases overall well-being.
5. **Boosts Job Satisfaction**: Maintaining a healthy balance leads to greater job satisfaction and a positive attitude towards your work.

Strategies to Achieve Work-Life Balance

1. **Set Clear Boundaries:** Establish clear boundaries between work and personal time. Communicate these boundaries to your colleagues and family to ensure mutual respect.

   - Define specific work hours and stick to them. Avoid checking work emails or taking work calls during personal time.

2. **Prioritise Tasks**: Focus on completing the most important tasks first. Prioritising helps you manage your workload more effectively and ensures that essential tasks are completed in a timely manner.

   - Use tools like to-do lists and time management apps to stay organised and prioritise tasks.

3. **Schedule Downtime:** Plan regular breaks and leisure activities to recharge. Scheduling downtime helps you relax and rejuvenate, improving your overall productivity.

   - Set aside time for hobbies, exercise, and social activities. Ensure you are completely free from work-related tasks at least one day a week.

4. **Learn to Say No:** Avoid overcommitting by learning to say no to additional tasks that do not align with your priorities. Setting limits helps prevent overload and stress.

   - Politely decline requests exceeding your capacity and focus on your responsibilities.

5. **Delegate Responsibilities: Share your workload by delegating tasks to colleagues or team members. Delegating ensures that you are not overwhelmed and allows others to contribute.**

   - Identify tasks others can handle and delegate accordingly, providing clear instructions and support as needed.

6. **Create a Dedicated Workspace**: If working from home, establish a dedicated workspace that separates work from personal life. A specific work area helps create a mental boundary between work and relaxation.

   - Set up a home office or a designated work corner, and avoid working from places associated with relaxation, such as your bed or couch.

7. **Practise Mindfulness**: Engage in mindfulness practises to stay present and focused. Mindfulness helps reduce stress and enhances your ability to manage work-life boundaries.

   - Incorporate practises such as meditation, deep breathing, and mindful walking into your daily routine.

8. **Take Care of Your Health**: Prioritise your physical and mental health through regular exercise, a balanced diet, and adequate sleep. Good health supports better work-life balance.

- Establish a regular exercise routine, eat nutritious meals, and ensure you get 7-8 hours of sleep each night.

9. **Disconnect Regularly**: Disconnect from digital devices and social media. Digital detoxes help you unwind and focus on personal interactions and activities.

   - Designate specific times for digital detox, such as during meals or before bedtime, and engage in offline activities.

10. **Seek Support**: Reach out for support from family, friends, or professional counsellors if needed. Support networks provide emotional assistance and practical advice for managing work-life balance.

    - Share your challenges with trusted individuals and seek their guidance and support.

Conclusion

Balancing work and life are crucial for maintaining health, productivity, and overall happiness. Here are key strategies to achieve a healthy work-life balance:

- Set clear boundaries

- Prioritise tasks

- Schedule downtime

- Learn to say no

- Delegate responsibilities

- Create a dedicated workspace

- Practise mindfulness

- Take care of your health

- Disconnect regularly

- Seek support

As Stephen Covey, author of "The 7 Habits of Highly Effective People," said, ***"The key is not to prioritise what's on your schedule, but to schedule your priorities."*** Embrace work-life balance, and you will enjoy a more fulfilling and productive life both professionally and personally.

Be Open to Feedback and Learning:

Embracing Growth and Improvement

Being open to feedback and willing to learn from it is crucial for personal and professional growth. Gracefully accepting constructive criticism and using it as a learning tool can significantly enhance your skills and performance. As Ken Blanchard, a renowned management expert, said, "Feedback is the breakfast of champions." Adopting this attitude fosters continuous improvement and development.

The Importance of Being Open to Feedback and Learning

1. **Fosters Growth**: Constructive feedback highlights areas for improvement and helps you grow personally and professionally.
2. **Enhances Performance**: Using feedback to make necessary adjustments can lead to better performance and higher quality work.
3. **Builds Resilience**: Accepting criticism gracefully strengthens your resilience and adaptability.
4. **Encourages Continuous Learning**: Openness to feedback promotes a mindset of continuous learning and self-improvement.
5. **Strengthens Relationships**: Valuing others' opinions and being receptive to their input builds trust and stronger professional relationships.

Strategies to Be Open to Feedback and Learning

1. **Adopt a Growth Mindset**: Embrace the belief that your abilities can develop through effort and learning. A growth mindset makes you more receptive to feedback.

   - View challenges and criticism as opportunities to learn and grow rather than as threats.

2. **Ask for Feedback**: Proactively seek feedback from supervisors, peers, and mentors. Regularly asking for input shows your commitment to improvement.

   - Schedule regular feedback sessions and ask specific questions to get detailed insights.

3. **Listen Actively**: When receiving feedback, listen without interrupting. Focus on understanding the message rather than formulating a response.

   - Take notes during feedback sessions to capture key points and reflect on them later.

4. **Stay Calm and Composed**: Maintain a calm and composed demeanour when receiving criticism. Avoid becoming defensive or emotional.

   - Take deep breaths and remind yourself that feedback is a tool for growth, not a personal attack.

5. **Seek Clarification**: If feedback is unclear, ask for clarification. Understanding the feedback fully is essential for applying it effectively.

   - Ask questions like, "Can you provide an example?" or "How can I improve in this area?"

6. **Reflect on Feedback**: Take time to reflect on the feedback you receive. Consider how it aligns with your goals and identify specific actions you can take.

   - Use a journal to document feedback and your reflections on how to apply it.

7. **Create an Action Plan**: Develop a clear plan to address the feedback. Set specific, measurable goals and outline steps to achieve them.

   - Break down larger goals into smaller, manageable tasks and set deadlines for each.

8. **Implement Changes**: Put your action plan into practise and make the necessary changes. Demonstrating that you can act on feedback shows your commitment to growth.

   - Monitor your progress and adjust your approach as needed to ensure continuous improvement.

9. **Follow-Up**: Arrange follow-up meetings with your feedback providers to discuss your progress and get additional input. Regular check-ins help keep you on track.

   - Use follow-up sessions to review your action plan, discuss challenges, and celebrate successes.

10. **Show Appreciation**: Thank those who provide you with feedback. Expressing gratitude reinforces positive relationships and encourages ongoing support.

- A simple thank-you note or verbal acknowledgement can go a long way in showing appreciation.

Conclusion

Being open to feedback and learning is essential for fostering growth and improvement. Here are key strategies to effectively use feedback to enhance your skills and performance:

- Adopt a growth mindset

- Ask for feedback

- Listen actively

- Stay calm and composed

- Seek clarification

- Reflect on feedback

- Create an action plan

- Implement changes

- Follow up

- Show appreciation

As **_Winston Churchill said, "To improve is to change; to be perfect is to change often."_** Embrace feedback and learning, and you will continuously grow and succeed personally and professionally.

Cultivate Problem-Solving Skills: Embracing a Solution-Oriented Mindset

Developing effective problem-solving skills is essential for success in any profession. A solution-oriented mindset enables you to approach challenges confidently and creatively, turning obstacles into opportunities for growth and improvement. As Albert Einstein famously said, ***"We cannot solve our problems with the same thinking we used when we created them."*** Cultivating problem-solving skills enhances your ability to navigate complex situations and deliver impactful results.

The Importance of Problem-Solving Skills

1. **Increases Efficiency**: Effective problem-solving helps identify and implement solutions quickly, improving overall efficiency.

2. **Enhances Decision-Making**: A structured approach to problem-solving leads to better, more informed decisions.

3. **Fosters Innovation**: Problem-solving encourages creative thinking and innovation, driving progress and competitive advantage.

4. **Builds Confidence**: Successfully resolving issues boosts confidence and empowers you to tackle future challenges.

5. **Strengthens Leadership**: Strong problem-solving skills are a hallmark of effective leaders, enhancing your ability to guide and support your team.

Strategies to Cultivate Problem-Solving Skills

1. **Adopt a Solution-Oriented Mindset**: Focus on finding solutions rather than dwelling on problems. A positive, proactive attitude is key to effective problem-solving.

   - Shift your perspective from "Why did this happen?" to "How can we fix this?"

2. **Define the Problem Clearly**: Accurately identify and define the problem. Understanding the root cause is crucial for developing effective solutions.

   - Use techniques like the "5 Whys" to drill down to the core issue.

3. **Gather Information**: Collect relevant data and information to understand the problem fully. Comprehensive information helps you make informed decisions.

   - Conduct research, seek stakeholder input, and analyse data for insights.

4. **Brainstorm Solutions**: Generate a list of potential solutions. Encourage creative thinking and consider all possibilities, even unconventional ones.

   - Use brainstorming techniques like mind mapping or the SCAMPER method to explore different ideas.

5. **Evaluate Options**: Assess each potential solution's feasibility, risks, and benefits. Consider factors such as resources, time, and impact.

- Create a pros and cons list or use decision-making tools like SWOT analysis to evaluate options.

6. **Develop an Action Plan**: Once you've selected the best solution, create a detailed action plan outlining the steps needed to implement it.

   - Set clear goals, assign responsibilities, and establish timelines to ensure effective execution.

7. **Implement the Solution**: Put your action plan into practice. Effective implementation requires coordination, communication, and monitoring.

   - Communicate the plan to all involved parties and track progress to ensure successful execution.

8. **Monitor and Adjust**: Continuously monitor the solution's effectiveness and be prepared to make adjustments as needed. Flexibility and adaptability are key to successful problem-solving.

   - Gather feedback, measure outcomes, and make necessary changes to improve the solution.

9. **Learn from Experience**: Reflect on the problem-solving process and outcomes. Identifying lessons learned helps you improve your skills and approach future challenges more effectively.

   - Document the process and outcomes, and conduct a post-mortem analysis to capture insights.

10. **Collaborate and Communicate**: Work with others to solve problems. Collaboration brings diverse

perspectives and expertise, enhancing the quality of solutions.

- Foster open communication, encourage teamwork and seek input from colleagues and stakeholders.

Conclusion

Cultivating problem-solving skills is essential for professional success and personal growth. Here are key strategies to navigate challenges with confidence and creativity:

- Adopt a solution-oriented mindset
- Define problems clearly
- Gather information
- Brainstorm solutions
- Evaluate options
- Develop action plans
- Implement solutions
- Monitor and adjust
- Learn from experience
- Collaborate and communicate effectively

As Charles F. Kettering said, **"A problem well stated is a problem half solved."** Embrace problem-solving, and you will enhance your ability to drive positive outcomes and achieve your goals.

Celebrate Small Wins: Boosting Morale and Motivation

Recognising and celebrating your achievements, no matter how small, is essential for maintaining high morale and motivation. Celebrating small wins helps you appreciate progress, reinforces positive behaviour, and motivates you to strive for success. As motivational speaker Tony Robbins said, "***The path to success is to take massive, determined action. But don't forget to celebrate the small wins along the way.***" Embracing this practice can significantly enhance your personal and professional journey.

The Importance of Celebrating Small Wins

1. **Boosts Morale**: Celebrating achievements, regardless of size, uplifts your spirits and boosts morale, creating a positive mindset.

2. **Increases Motivation**: Recognising progress motivates and encourages you to continue working towards your goals.

3. **Reinforces Positive Behaviour**: Celebrating successes reinforces the behaviours and actions that led to those achievements, encouraging you to repeat them.

4. **Reduces Stress**: Taking time to celebrate reduces stress and provides a moment to relax and recharge.

5. **Enhances Well-Being**: Celebrating small wins contributes to overall happiness and well-being by fostering a sense of accomplishment and satisfaction.

Strategies to Celebrate Small Wins

1. **Acknowledge Your Achievements**: Take a moment to recognise and appreciate your accomplishments, no matter how minor they may seem. Acknowledgement is the first step in celebrating.

   - Keep a journal to note your achievements and reflect on them regularly.

2. **Share with Others**: Share your successes with friends, family, or colleagues. Celebrating together enhances the joy and provides additional motivation.

   - Share your wins with social media, team meetings, or personal conversations.

3. **Reward Yourself**: Treat yourself to something special as a reward for your hard work. Rewards provide a tangible recognition of your efforts.

   - Choose meaningful rewards, such as a favourite meal, a relaxing day off, or a new book.

4. **Reflect on Your Progress**: Take time to reflect on your progress towards your larger goals. Reflecting helps you see how small wins contribute to your overall success.

   - Create a visual representation of your progress, such as a chart or checklist, to track and celebrate each step.

5. **Set Milestones**: Break down your larger goals into smaller, achievable milestones. Each milestone provides

an opportunity to celebrate and recognise your progress.

- Clearly define each milestone and plan a celebration for when you achieve it.

6. **Create a Celebration Ritual**: Establish a regular ritual for celebrating small wins. Rituals help you develop a consistent habit of recognising and appreciating your achievements.

- For example, end each week by listing three accomplishments and treating yourself to a small reward.

7. **Encourage Others**: Celebrate your colleagues' and team members' small wins. Encouraging others creates a positive and supportive work environment.

- Offer praise, recognition, and small tokens of appreciation for others' achievements.

8. **Keep a Success Wall**: Create a physical or digital space where you display your achievements. A success wall serves as a constant reminder of your progress and accomplishments.

- Showcase your successes on a bulletin board, a section of your office wall, or a digital document.

9. **Reflect on Challenges Overcome**: Recognise your achievements and the challenges you've overcome. Celebrating your resilience and perseverance is equally important.

- Write down the obstacles you've faced and how you overcame them, and take pride in your resilience.

10. **Stay Present**: Focus on the present moment and enjoy the feelings of accomplishment. Staying present helps you fully appreciate your successes without immediately shifting focus to the next goal.

- Practise mindfulness techniques to stay grounded and fully experience your celebrations.

Conclusion

Celebrating small wins is essential for maintaining morale, motivation, and overall well-being. Here are key strategies to effectively celebrate your successes:

- Acknowledge your achievements
- Share with others
- Reward yourself
- Reflect on your progress
- Set milestones
- Create celebration rituals
- Encourage others
- Keep a success wall
- Reflect on challenges overcome
- Stay present

Oprah Winfrey wisely said, ***"The more you praise and celebrate your life, the more there is in life to celebrate."*** Embrace the practice of celebrating small wins, and you will foster a positive, motivated, and successful personal and professional life.

The Importance of Letting Go: Embracing Freedom and Growth

Letting go is an essential aspect of personal and professional growth. It involves releasing negative emotions, unhelpful habits, and limiting beliefs that hold you back. Letting go creates space for new opportunities, positive experiences, and personal development. As Buddha wisely said, "You only lose what you cling to." Embracing letting go can lead to a more fulfilling and liberated life.

The Importance of Letting Go

1. **Reduces Stress and Anxiety**: Holding onto past grievances and worries creates unnecessary stress and anxiety. Letting go helps you find peace and reduces mental burden.
2. **Promotes Emotional Healing**: Releasing negative emotions and past traumas allows for emotional healing and recovery, fostering a healthier mindset.
3. **Enhances Personal Growth**: Letting go of limiting beliefs and self-doubt encourages personal growth and self-improvement.
4. **Improves Relationships**: Releasing grudges and resentments improves your relationships by fostering forgiveness and understanding.
5. **Increases Resilience**: Letting go of the need for control builds resilience and adaptability, helping you navigate life's challenges more effectively.

6. **Boosts Happiness and Well-being**: Letting go of what no longer serves you enhances overall happiness and well-being by allowing you to focus on the present and future.

Strategies to Practise Letting Go

1. **Acknowledge Your Feelings: Recognise and accept your emotions instead of suppressing them. Acknowledgement is the first step towards letting go.**

   - Practise journaling or talking to a trusted friend to process your emotions.

2. **Practise Mindfulness: Mindfulness helps you stay present and observe your thoughts without judgment. It allows you to release negative thoughts and focus on the here and now.**

   - Incorporate mindfulness meditation or deep breathing exercises into your daily routine.

3. **Forgive Yourself and Others: Forgiveness is crucial for letting go. It involves releasing feelings of anger and resentment towards yourself and others.**

   - Reflect on the benefits of forgiveness and actively choose to forgive, even if it takes time.

4. **Focus on What You Can Control: Let go of the need to control everything. Focus on what you can influence and accept what you cannot change.**

   - Make a list of things within your control and those outside your control to gain perspective.

5. **Set Boundaries: Establish healthy boundaries to protect your well-being. Letting go of toxic relationships and situations is vital for personal growth.**

   - Communicate your boundaries clearly and enforce them consistently.

6. **Embrace Change: Accept that change is a natural part of life. Letting go of the past allows you to embrace new opportunities and experiences.**

   - Remind yourself that change often leads to growth and new possibilities.

7. **Seek Support: Surround yourself with supportive friends, family, or professionals who can help you through the process of letting go.**

   - Consider joining support groups or seeking therapy for additional guidance.

8. **Reframe Negative Thoughts: Challenge and reframe negative thoughts and beliefs that hold you back. Replace them with positive and empowering affirmations.**

   - Practise positive self-talk and affirmations to build a more positive mindset.

9. **Focus on Personal Growth: Engage in activities that promote personal growth and self-improvement. This shifts your focus from the past to your potential.**

- Pursue hobbies, courses, or projects that inspire and challenge you.

10. **Celebrate Your Progress**: Acknowledge and celebrate your progress in letting go. Recognising your achievements boosts motivation and confidence.

- Keep a journal of your journey and reflect on how far you've come.

Conclusion

- Letting go is a powerful practice that promotes emotional healing, personal growth, and overall well-being. Here are key strategies to effectively let go of what no longer serves you:

- Acknowledge your feelings

- Practise mindfulness

- Forgive yourself and others

- Focus on what you can control

- Set boundaries

- Embrace change

- Seek support

- Reframe negative thoughts

- Focus on personal growth

- Celebrate your progress

As Lao Tzu said, **_"When I let go of what I am, I become what I might be."_** Embrace the importance of letting go, and you will find freedom, growth, and a more fulfilling life.

Take Nothing for Granted: Embrace the Preciousness of Every Moment

Life is an extraordinary gift, brimming with beauty and moments of joy, yet we often fall into the trap of taking it for granted. We assume our loved ones will always be by our side and that our health and happiness are constants. However, the reality is that life is both impermanent and unpredictable. Reflecting on the carefree days of childhood, those seemingly endless joyful moments, helps us realise how precious those times truly were. Now, they are cherished memories, reminding us to treasure the present.

The Impermanence of Life

Understanding Life's Fragility

Life's transience is a fundamental truth we often overlook. We assume permanence in our relationships, health, and circumstances. But life can change in an instant. Recognising this fragility helps us appreciate the present more deeply.

"Life is short, and it's up to you to make it sweet." — Sarah Louise Delany.

Cherishing Childhood Memories

Remember the carefree days of your childhood? Running and playing with friends, those joyful moments seemed endless. Now, they are treasured memories, reminding us to value the present. Childhood memories serve as a poignant reminder of life's fleeting nature.

Expressing Gratitude: The Power of Gratitude

Gratitude is a powerful tool for transforming how we perceive and experience life. By expressing gratitude, we shift our focus from what we lack to what we have, fostering a sense of fulfilment and joy.

Example: Keep a gratitude journal. Each day, jot down three things you are grateful for. This practice can significantly enhance your appreciation for the little things.

Actions to Implement Gratitude

1. **Daily Gratitude Journaling**: Spend a few minutes each day writing about things you are thankful for. This habit can help cultivate a positive outlook on life.
2. **Verbalise Your Appreciation**: Regularly tell your loved ones how much you appreciate them. It can strengthen your relationships and create a positive environment.

Savouring the Present Moment

Living in the Now

To truly live, we must immerse ourselves in the present. Savouring the present moment means appreciating what is happening right now rather than dwelling on the past or worrying about the future.

"Do not dwell in the past, do not dream of the future, concentrate the mind on the present moment." — Buddha

Actions to Stay Present

1. **Mindfulness Meditation**: Practise mindfulness meditation to anchor yourself in the present. Focus on your breath and the sensations around you.
2. **Disconnect to Reconnect**: Take regular breaks from technology. Spend time in nature, read a book, or have a meaningful conversation without distractions.

Appreciating Loved Ones

Treasuring Relationships

Our relationships are among the most significant aspects of our lives. Cherish the laughter you share with your siblings, the unconditional love of your parents, and the moments of connection with friends and partners.

Example: Make a habit of regular family dinners or weekly calls with distant relatives. These small acts help maintain strong bonds and create lasting memories.

Actions to Strengthen Relationships

1. **Quality Time**: Dedicate uninterrupted time to your loved ones. Engage in activities that strengthen your bond.
2. **Express Love and Affection**: Don't wait until it's too late to show your love. A simple hug, a kind word, or a thoughtful gesture can go a long way.

Finding Joy in Small Things

Embracing Simple Pleasures

Life is composed of countless small moments that bring joy. A beautiful sunset, a delicious meal, or a kind gesture from a stranger—these are the moments that make life beautiful and meaningful.

"Enjoy the little things, for one day you may look back and realise they were the big things." — Robert Brault

Actions to Enjoy Simple Pleasures

1. **Daily Walks**: Take a daily walk and appreciate your surroundings. Notice the colours, sounds, and smells that you might usually overlook.
2. **Mindful Eating**: Savour each bite of your meals. Pay attention to the Flavors, textures, and aromas. This practice can make eating a more joyful experience.

Living with Presence and Awe

Cultivating a Sense of Wonder

Living with a sense of awe and presence means recognising the miracle of your existence. Approach each day with curiosity and wonder, and you'll find beauty in the ordinary.

Example: Practise gratitude walks. As you walk, think about the things you are grateful for. This can help you feel more connected to your surroundings and the present moment.

Actions to Cultivate Awe

1. **Explore Nature**: Spend time in nature to experience its beauty and complexity. Whether it's a hike, a visit to the beach, or simply a walk in the park, nature instils awe.
2. **Learn Something New**: Engage in lifelong learning. Take up a new hobby, learn a new skill, or explore a new topic. This keeps life exciting and fosters a sense of wonder.

Practising Presence in Daily Life

Integrating Mindfulness into Daily Activities

Mindfulness doesn't have to be confined to meditation sessions. Integrate mindfulness into daily activities like washing dishes, driving, or working. Focus fully on the task at hand.

Example: When washing dishes, pay attention to the feel of the water, the texture, and the sounds around you. This can transform a mundane task into a mindful practice.

Actions to Practise Daily Mindfulness

1. **Mindful Mornings**: Start your day with a few minutes of mindfulness. Set an intention for the day and focus on your breath.

2. **Mindful Breaks**: Take short mindfulness breaks throughout the day. Close your eyes, take a few deep breaths, and bring awareness to the present moment.

Conclusion

Embracing the preciousness of every moment is a journey that requires conscious effort and practice. You can transform your life by understanding life's impermanence, expressing gratitude, savouring the present, appreciating loved ones, finding joy in small things, living with presence, and practising mindfulness in daily activities. Start today to see the blessings all around you truly. Live each day with presence, love, and awe at the miracle of your existence. Take nothing for granted; you will discover the richness and wonder of being alive.

Remember, it's not about waiting for a tragedy to wake you up; it's about starting now to cherish every moment. Your journey to a more mindful and grateful life begins today.

Actions to Implement These Principles as a Habit

1. **Daily Gratitude Practice**: Keep a journal and write down three things you are grateful for daily.
2. **Mindfulness Meditation**: Dedicate 10 minutes each day to mindfulness meditation.
3. **Quality Time with Loved Ones**: Schedule regular time for family and friends.
4. **Appreciate Simple Pleasures**: Take daily walks and savour your meals.

5. **Cultivate Awe**: Spend time in nature and learn something new regularly.
6. **Mindful Integration**: Practise mindfulness during daily activities and take mindful breaks.

Incorporating these actions into your daily routine will foster a deeper appreciation for life and its myriad moments.

You Deserve the Best! Prioritise Self-Love and Self-Care!

You are a magnificent, one-of-a-kind individual worthy of the utmost love and care. Yet so often, we neglect ourselves while pouring our energy into others. It's time to flip the script and make yourself the number one priority! When did you last take a luxurious bubble bath? Or have you savoured a delicious meal without distractions? Prioritise regular self-care rituals that nourish your body, mind, and soul. Get a massage, take a yoga class, or go for a nature walk. Recharge your batteries so you can show up as your best self. Remember, self-love and self-care are not selfish acts but essential practices that enable you to give your best to others.

The Importance of Self-Love

Acknowledging Your Worth

Recognise that you are deserving of love and care simply because you exist. Your value is inherent, and you do not need to earn it. This realisation forms the foundation of self-love. Look in the mirror and tell yourself, "I love you!"

Appreciate your unique features and your beautiful body. You are a masterpiece, exactly as you are.

Banishing the Inner Critic

We all have an inner critic that can be harsh and unforgiving. It's time to silence those critical voices and replace them with compassion. Instead of focusing on perceived flaws, celebrate your strengths and achievements. You are enough, always.

Practising Self-Care

Establishing Self-Care Rituals

Regular self-care rituals are vital for maintaining your well-being. These rituals can be as simple as taking a bubble bath, reading a book, or enjoying a cup of tea without distractions. The key is to do something that brings you joy and relaxation.

Examples of Self-Care Activities

1. **Luxurious Bubble Bath**: Set time for a long, relaxing bath. Use your favourite bath salts or oils, light some candles, and let the warm water soothe your body and mind.
2. **Savour a Meal**: Prepare your favourite meal and savour every bite. Turn off the TV, put away your phone, and focus on the flavours and textures of the food.
3. **Get a Massage**: Treat yourself to a professional massage. This can help relieve stress and tension, leaving you feeling refreshed and rejuvenated.

4. **Take a Yoga Class**: Yoga is a great way to connect with your body and mind. It helps reduce stress, increase flexibility, and promote overall well-being.

5. **Nature Walk**: Spend time in nature to recharge your batteries. Whether it's a walk in the park or a hike in the mountains, being in nature can help you feel grounded and rejuvenated.

The Power of Affirmations

Using Positive Affirmations

Positive affirmations are powerful tools for cultivating self-love. Repeating affirmations can reprogram your mind to focus on positive beliefs about yourself. Examples of affirmations include:

- I am worthy of love and respect.
- I am enough, just as I am.
- I deserve happiness and success.
- I am proud of who I am becoming.

Incorporating Affirmations into Your Routine

Incorporate affirmations into your daily routine by writing them down, saying them aloud, or placing them in visible locations. Over time, these affirmations can help build a positive self-image and boost your self-esteem.

Self-Love as a Lifelong Journey

Commitment to Self-Improvement

Self-love is not a destination but a lifelong journey. It requires a commitment to continually nurturing and improving yourself. Embrace the process and be patient with yourself as you grow and evolve.

Setting Boundaries

Part of self-love involves setting healthy boundaries. Learn to say no to things that drain your energy and yes to activities that nourish your soul. Respecting your own needs and limits is crucial for maintaining your well-being.

Conclusion

When you prioritise self-love and self-care, you send a powerful message to the universe: You are worthy. You matter. And from this place of self-acceptance and self-respect, you can share your gifts with the world in a way no one else can. Embrace the awesomeness that is you!

Spread Sunshine with Heartfelt Compliments!

Imagine the impact you could have made if you had learned the power of sincere, specific compliments at a younger age. The lives you could have uplifted, the relationships you could have deepened, the confidence you could have instilled in others. It's always possible to start making a difference with your words.

Take a moment to think about the people in your life — your spouse, children, coworkers, and neighbours. What unique qualities do you admire in them? What small acts of kindness or achievements have you noticed? Don't keep those thoughts to yourself — share them!

The Power of a Compliment

Transforming Relationships

Compliments are like sunshine on a cloudy day; they have the power to transform relationships. By acknowledging and appreciating the positive traits and actions of those around you, you can create stronger, more meaningful connections. A simple, heartfelt compliment can turn someone's entire day around. It costs nothing, yet the impact is priceless.

Boosting Confidence

When you give someone a sincere compliment, you boost their confidence. They feel seen, valued, and appreciated.

This boost in confidence can motivate them to keep going, try harder, and believe in themselves more.

Fostering Positivity

Compliments foster positivity. They create a ripple effect; the person you compliment feels good and is likelier to pass on that positivity to others. This chain reaction can create a more positive and uplifting environment for everyone.

Crafting the Perfect Compliment

Be Specific

Specific compliments are more impactful than general ones. Instead of saying, "You're great," try, "I really admire how you handled that difficult situation with grace and patience." Specific compliments show that you are paying attention and truly appreciate the person's efforts.

Be Sincere

Sincerity is key. People can tell when a compliment is genuine or just flattery. Make sure your compliments are heartfelt and based on true observations.

Be Timely

Strike when the moment is right. A timely compliment can be more meaningful than one given much later. For example, complimenting your partner on a delicious meal right after dinner will likely have a greater impact than mentioning it the next day.

Putting It into Practice

Complimenting Your Spouse

Imagine the smile that would light up your partner's face if you complimented the delicious meal they prepared. Try saying, "This meal is fantastic! You really outdid yourself. I love how you used those spices."

Praising Your Children

Picture the pride in your child's eyes when you praise their hard work on a school project. You might say, "I'm so impressed by the effort you put into this project. Your creativity and dedication really shine through."

Acknowledging Your Coworkers

Envision the boost in your colleague's morale when you acknowledge their contributions. A comment like, "Your presentation today was spot on. You really captured the client's needs and provided great solutions," can make a huge difference.

Appreciating Your Neighbours

Don't forget about your neighbours. A simple, "I really appreciate how you always keep your garden looking so beautiful. It brightens up the whole street" can foster community and goodwill.

The Joy of Giving Compliments

Become a Praise Ninja

Embrace the joy of being a "praise ninja" — strike when they least expect it with a thoughtful, specific compliment that leaves them beaming. The more you give, the more the world will shine.

Notice the Good

Start noticing the good in those around you. The more you focus on positive qualities and actions, the more you will see. This shift in perspective can make you a more positive and appreciative person overall.

Spread Positivity

Your words have the power to uplift, inspire, and transform lives. Spread sunshine with your heartfelt compliments. The more you give, the more positivity you will create.

Conclusion

Heartfelt compliments are powerful tools for building stronger relationships, boosting confidence, and fostering positivity. By noticing and appreciating the good in others, you can create a more uplifting and positive environment. So, don't wait—start spreading sunshine today with your sincere, specific compliments. Your words can make a world of difference.

Unleash Your Inner Dancer and Embrace Life!

Imagine you had the wisdom to stop sitting on the sidelines and start dancing through life. What adventures would you have embarked on? What dreams would you have chased? What connections would you have forged? It's never too late to shed your inhibitions and dive headfirst into the rhythm of life.

Picture yourself swaying to the beat of the music, lost in the moment, your body moving with joyful abandon. Or imagine yourself tackling a new challenge, learning a new skill, and exploring uncharted territory — all with a spirit of playful curiosity. When you actively participate in life, the world becomes your dance floor. Gone are the days of passively watching from the sidelines, envious of those living their best lives. Now, you're taking centre stage, embracing each moment with open arms.

Stepping Out of Your Comfort Zone

Embrace the Uncomfortable

Stepping out of your comfort zone is never easy, but that's where the magic happens. It might feel awkward at first to dance like no one is watching, but with each spin, each leap, and each improvised move, you'll discover newfound confidence, creativity, and a zest for living that will inspire everyone around you.

"Life begins at the end of your comfort zone." — Neale Donald Walsch

Start small by trying something new every week. It could be as simple as taking a different route to work, joining a new class, or speaking to someone new. Each small step outside your comfort zone builds your confidence.

Embracing Joyful Movement

Dance with Abandon

There's something liberating about dancing with joyful abandon. It's a physical expression of freedom and joy. Imagine yourself in your living room, the music turned up loud, and you're dancing like no one is watching. Feel the music pulse through your veins, and let your body move without judgment.

Example: Put on your favourite song and dance for five minutes daily. Notice how it uplifts your mood and energises your spirit.

Sign up for a dance class or join a local dance group. The structured setting can help you learn new moves and meet new people while dancing itself will boost your mood and confidence.

Tackling New Challenges

Cultivate Playful Curiosity

Life is full of opportunities to learn and grow. Embrace a spirit of playful curiosity by tackling new challenges and learning new skills. Whether you pick up a musical instrument, learn a new language, or try a new hobby, let your curiosity guide you.

"We keep moving forward, opening new doors, and doing new things because we're curious, and curiosity keeps leading us down new paths." — Walt Disney

Choose one new skill or hobby you've always wanted to try and dedicate weekly time to practise it. Celebrate your progress, no matter how small.

Building Meaningful Connections

Forge New Relationships

Dancing through life means forging new connections and deepening existing ones. Be open to meeting new people and forming meaningful relationships. Engage in conversations, listen actively, and share your stories and experiences.

Example: Attend local events or join clubs and groups that interest you. These settings provide opportunities to meet like-minded individuals and build connections.

Action: Try to reconnect with old friends or family members you haven't spoken to. A simple message or phone call can rekindle relationships and create new memories.

Living with Passion and Purpose

Take Center Stage

Stop being a spectator in your own life. Take centre stage and live with passion and purpose. Pursue your dreams with vigour, and don't be afraid to take risks. The world is your stage, and it's time to shine.

"The only way to do great work is to love what you do." — Steve Jobs

Identify your passion and find ways to incorporate it into your daily life. Whether through your career, hobbies, or volunteer work, make sure you're dedicating time to what you love.

Conclusion

Life is meant to be danced, not just observed. You can transform your life into a vibrant dance by stepping out of your comfort zone, embracing joyful movement, tackling new challenges, building meaningful connections, and living with passion and purpose. So, crank up the music, kick off your shoes, and let your body lead the way. What are you waiting for? The dance floor is yours!

Embrace the rhythm of life and watch as your confidence, creativity, and joy soar. The adventures you've dreamed of are within reach, the dreams you've held onto are ready to be chased, and the connections you've longed for are waiting to be forged. Unleash your inner dancer and embrace life fully.

Embrace the Abundance of Who You Are!

Imagine having the wisdom to know you are already enough and possess all the resources, talents, and potential you need to live a fulfilling life. How would that have transformed your journey? Too often, we get caught up in the relentless pursuit of more, more money, more success, and more possessions. But the true path to happiness lies in cultivating a mindset of abundance, self-acceptance, and self-worth.

Embrace Self-Worth and Abundance

Understanding Your Inherent Worth

Repeat after me: "I have enough. I am enough. I do enough." Let those words sink in, and feel their weight lift from your shoulders. You are a unique, irreplaceable individual worthy of love and respect, just as you are. Embracing this mindset can profoundly change your interactions with the world and yourself.

"You are enough just as you are." — Meghan Markle

Silencing the Inner Critic

Banish Negative Self-Talk

We all have that critical inner voice that tells us we're not good, capable, or deserving. It's time to silence that voice and replace it with affirmations celebrating your strengths, resilience, and capacity for growth.

Action: Whenever you catch yourself thinking negatively, stop and reframe the thought. Instead of "I can't do this," tell yourself, "I am capable and can handle challenges."

Surrounding Yourself with Positivity

Build a Supportive Network

Surround yourself with people who see your true worth and uplift you. Positive relationships are crucial for maintaining a healthy mindset. These people remind you of your values and encourage you to pursue your dreams.

Example: Seek friends, mentors, or communities that inspire and support you. Engage in activities that foster positive interactions and personal growth.

Cultivating a Mindset of Abundance

Recognise What You Have

When you operate from a place of abundance, the world opens up to you. Doors of opportunity swing wide, relationships deepen, and your impact expands. You no longer need to prove your value — you effortlessly radiate it.

Practise gratitude daily. Reflect on what you are thankful for and acknowledge the abundance already present in your life. This can be done through journaling, meditation, or simply a moment of reflection each day.

"Gratitude turns what we have into enough." — Anonymous

Living with Abundance

Take Risks and Chase Dreams

Imagine the life you could have lived if you had embraced this mindset at a very young age. The risks you would have taken, the dreams you would have chased, the lives you would have touched. It's never too late to start. Your abundance awaits — all you have to do is claim it.

Identify one dream or goal you've been hesitant to pursue. Take a small step towards it today. Whether it's signing up for a class, reaching out to a potential mentor, or simply making a plan, start moving towards your dream.

Affirmations for Abundance

Incorporate Daily Affirmations

Use affirmations to reinforce your mindset of abundance and self-worth. Affirmations are powerful tools that can reshape your thinking and help you focus on your inherent worth and potential.

Examples of Affirmations:

- I am worthy of all the good things life has to offer.
- I trust in my ability to create a wonderful life.
- I am surrounded by love and abundance.
- My potential is limitless, and I embrace it fully.

Conclusion

Embracing the abundance of who you are is a journey of self-discovery and acceptance. By understanding your inherent worth, silencing your inner critic, surrounding yourself with positivity, and cultivating a mindset of abundance, you unlock the potential to live a life full of joy, fulfilment, and impact. It's never too late to start. Embrace your abundance today, and watch as the world opens up to you in ways you never imagined.

Your abundance awaits — all you have to do is claim it.

Cultivating Positive Digital Habits

Cultivating positive digital habits is like gardening in the wild jungle of the internet. You need to prune the excess, water the plants of knowledge, and pull up the weeds of distractions. Imagine your social media feed as a garden plot — left unchecked, it can quickly become overrun with useless information and negativity. With a little effort, you can transform it into a flourishing haven filled with content that nurtures your growth and keeps you motivated. By mindfully selecting what you consume and setting boundaries on screen time, you'll find yourself more productive, less stressed, and more energised to tackle your goals.

Mindful Consumption of Digital Media

Curating Your Digital Garden

In today's fast-paced digital world, the sheer volume of daily content can be overwhelming. From social media updates to breaking news, our screens are constantly filled with information. However, mindlessly scrolling and consuming digital media can hinder personal growth and success. It is essential to cultivate mindful consumption habits to ensure that the content we engage with contributes positively to our lives.

Intentional Selection of Content: Instead of allowing algorithms to dictate what you see, take control and curate your feed. Consider unfollowing accounts that don't add value or cause unnecessary stress and instead follow those that inspire growth and positivity. This way, you are the one who decides what you see when you open your social media apps, ensuring that you are greeted with content that fuels your ambition and well-being rather than draining it.

Setting Boundaries for Screen Time

Establishing Screen Time Limits: It's easy to lose track of time when engrossed in a fascinating article or entertaining video, but excessive screen time can lead to burnout and decreased productivity. By establishing specific times of the day to check your devices and sticking to them, you are taking responsibility for your digital habits. For example, you could designate morning breakfast and post-dinner as your catch-up times, giving yourself tech-free periods to focus on other tasks and mental relaxation.

Purposeful Engagement

Active Participation: It's not just about what you consume but how you interact with it. When reading an article or watching a video, try to absorb the information critically and reflect on how it relates to your goals. Engage with the content by taking notes, sharing thoughts with friends, or journaling about your learning. This active participation ensures enriching online time and supports continuous personal development.

Diversifying Your Digital Diet

Avoiding Echo Chambers: Relying on a single source of information can create echo chambers that limit exposure to different viewpoints. Make a conscious effort to explore various platforms and types of content, from podcasts and blogs to documentaries and webinars. This broader perspective will enhance your knowledge and encourage critical thinking and empathy by considering multiple sides of an issue.

Embracing Digital Detoxes

Regular Breaks from Devices: Regular breaks from your devices can help reset your mind and reduce digital fatigue. Schedule short daily detoxes, such as during meals or before bed, and longer breaks during weekends or vacations. Use this offline time to connect with nature, pursue hobbies, or spend quality moments with loved ones. These breaks can rejuvenate you and provide clarity, making your return to the digital world more focused and intentional.

Quality Over Quantity

Deep Engagement with Content: With so much content available, it's tempting to skim through as much as possible, but this often leads to superficial understanding. Instead, choose a few interesting pieces and delve into them deeply. Read books by experts in your field, watch in-depth interviews, and look for comprehensive analyses. This approach will enable you to better understand and apply the knowledge to your personal growth journey.

Emotional Impact of Digital Content

Balancing Emotional Responses: Some media can evoke strong emotions like fear, anger, or sadness, negatively affecting your mood and mental health. After engaging with different types of content, pay attention to how you feel and try to balance it with positive and uplifting material. Following motivational speakers, educational content, or humour pages can counterbalance the more stressful aspects of your digital experience.

Self-Reflection on Digital Consumption

Weekly Review and Adjustment: Developing a habit of self-reflection regarding your digital consumption can be transformative. At the end of each week, take a moment to review what you've consumed and its effects on your life. Ask yourself, "What content was most valuable?" and "Did anything I read or watch help me achieve my goals?" This practice holds you accountable and guides future consumption choices toward more constructive and beneficial directions.

Practising Gratitude

Mindfulness and Appreciation: Mindful consumption extends beyond choosing and reflecting on content; it includes practising gratitude and mindfulness while engaging with digital media. Focus on being present and appreciative of the opportunities technology provides. Recognise the privilege of accessing vast resources and communities at your fingertips. Fostering a sense of gratitude will likely bring greater joy and meaning to your digital interactions.

Building a Digital Organisation System

Structuring Your Digital Files

Organising Your Digital Workspace: In this digital age, having an organised virtual workspace is just as crucial as keeping your physical desk tidy. Imagine entering a clutter-free office where everything you need is within arm's reach — that's the goal for your digital files and tasks. Start by creating broad folders for significant categories such as Work, Personal, Finances, etc. Within these, subfolders like "Reports," "Invoices," or "Emails" can help narrow things down further. Consistency in naming conventions is critical here. Stick to clear, specific names like "2021 Q3 Financial Report" instead of vague titles like "Report." This way, you don't have to rummage through ambiguously named files when looking for something specific.

Utilising Shortcuts and Tags

Efficient Access to Files: Shortcuts and tags can save space and hassle. Shortcuts allow quick access to frequently used files without duplicating them. Tags add another layer of searchability; for instance, tagging files with keywords like "urgent," "pending," or "reference" can make it easier to retrieve them later. These small steps can significantly streamline your digital environment, making it organised and incredibly efficient.

Organising Tasks

Digital Task Management Tools: Digital task management tools like Trello, Asana, or even simple Google Sheets can be game-changers. Rather than scribbling to-dos on random sticky notes or jotting them down in multiple apps, consolidating tasks in one place can provide visibility and control. Start with a basic setup. Create columns for To-Do, In Progress, and Done, giving each task a card to move through these stages. Using deadlines and priorities within these tools can further boost efficiency. Assign due dates and flag essential tasks to see what needs immediate attention and can wait. Colour-coding tasks are another way to visualise workloads better. Green might signify tasks nearing completion, while red could indicate those needing urgent action.

Effective Email Management

Achieving Inbox Zero: A cluttered inbox can quickly become overwhelming, leading to missed messages and delayed responses. One strategy is to implement the "Inbox Zero" philosophy — always aiming to keep your inbox nearly empty. This doesn't mean responding to every email immediately, but organising them effectively. Create folders or labels such as "Action Required," "Waiting for Response," and "Archive." Use filters to automatically sort incoming emails into these categories based on defined criteria. Unsubscribe from newsletters and spam that no longer serve you to reduce incoming clutter. Regularly allocating time to process your inbox — say 15 minutes each morning and afternoon — can keep things manageable.

Organising Digital Bookmarks

Streamlining Your Browser: Organising digital bookmarks and shortcuts also contributes to a more streamlined digital experience. Browsers like Chrome or Firefox enable you to create folders within your bookmarks bar. Categorise websites you visit frequently into groups like News, Work Tools, Learning Resources, etc. This prevents your bookmark bar from becoming a chaotic mess of links. Periodically review and clean up your bookmarks. Delete obsolete links and update outdated ones. Pinning essential tabs ensures they're easily accessible without constantly searching for them. Browser extensions like OneTab can consolidate many open tabs into one list, reducing clutter and improving performance.

Maintaining Digital Organisation

Regular Upkeep and Automation: Like any good habit, staying organised digitally requires regular upkeep. Set aside time weekly or monthly for digital cleaning sessions. During these sessions, declutter unnecessary files, reorganise misplaced items, and back up critical documents. Treat these sessions like a routine check-up for your digital health. Use automated tools wherever possible. Software that automatically backs up files clears temporary data, and updates apps can save significant manual effort. Automation can benefit repetitive tasks like file archiving or data syncing across devices. The less manual intervention required, the smoother your digital life becomes.

Maintaining Digital Health and Well-being

Managing Screen Time

Wise Screen Time Management: In today's digital age, fostering practices that promote digital well-being is essential for personal growth and success. The first step to achieving digital well-being is managing screen time wisely. While spending hours scrolling through social media or binge-watching series is tempting, setting boundaries can make a difference. Allocate specific times for recreational screen use and stick to them. For example, designate one hour in the evening to relax with your favourite show or catch up on social media. This practice helps prevent burnout and ensures that digital consumption remains a pleasure rather than a stress source.

Regular Breaks from Devices

Incorporating Breaks: Incorporating regular breaks from your devices is crucial. Staring at screens for extended periods can strain your eyes and negatively impact your mental health. The 20–20–20 rule is a helpful guideline: every 20 minutes, take a 20-second break to look at something 20 feet away. Incorporating brief pauses allows you to rest your eyes and reset your focus. During these breaks, consider engaging in offline activities such as stretching, walking, or meditating. This not only rejuvenates your mind but also fosters a balanced lifestyle.

Creating Tech-Free Zones

Tech-Free Times and Zones: Creating a tech-free zone or time within your daily routine can significantly enhance digital well-being. Designate specific areas, like the dining table, as gadget-free zones, or set specific hours during which devices are put away. For instance, establish a no-screen policy during meals or before bedtime. Doing so encourages meaningful face-to-face interactions and provides a much-needed break from the constant influx of digital information. It's incredible how much more connected and refreshed you'll feel by simply unplugging periodically.

Curating a Positive Digital Environment

Mindful Content Selection: Curating a positive digital environment starts with being mindful of the content you consume and the people you interact with online. Evaluate whether the websites, social media pages, and forums you frequent contribute to or detract from your well-being. Unfollow accounts that cause unnecessary stress or negativity and seek out sources that inspire and educate. Surrounding yourself with uplifting digital content can significantly improve your mood and outlook.

Managing Your Digital Footprint

Conscious Sharing: Be conscientious about your digital footprint. Be aware of what you post and share online. Before hitting "send" on a message or upload, ask yourself if it adds value to your or others' lives. Negative interactions and impulsive sharing can lead to regrets and affect your reputation. Remember, once something is online, it's there to stay. You maintain a positive presence and contribute to a healthier online community by posting thoughtfully.

Effective Notification Management

Prioritising Notifications: Constant pings and alerts can be distracting and overwhelming. Customise notification settings to prioritise what's most important. Turn off non-essential notifications and set specific times to check emails and messages. This reduces interruptions and allows you to focus on meaningful tasks. Controlling the influx of information creates a more serene and productive digital space.

Practising Mindful Digital Consumption

Identifying Time-Wasters: Developing healthy habits around digital consumption involves practising mindful use of technology. Start by identifying your main digital time-wasters. Recognising these pitfalls, whether endless scrolling through social media feeds or getting lost in YouTube videos, is critical. Set limits on how long you engage in these activities. You can use built-in tools on your smartphone or third-party apps to monitor and control your usage. Mindfulness in this context means being present and intentional about your digital interactions.

Engaging with Educational Content

Diversifying Online Activities: Alongside mindful usage, diversify your online activities with educational and enriching content. There is a wealth of resources online that can aid personal development, from free courses and webinars to informative podcasts and insightful articles. Make it a habit to replace some leisure time with learning. For instance, commit to watching a TED Talk or reading an article related to your interests daily. Engaging with content that stimulates your mind can transform your digital time into an opportunity for growth.

Establishing Digital Detox Routines

Regular Detoxes: Establishing a consistent digital detox routine is invaluable for maintaining balance. Dedicate time each week to completely disconnect from all digital devices. Whether it's an hour each day or a full day over the weekend, find what works best for you. Use this time to reconnect with nature, enjoy hobbies, or spend quality time with loved ones. Regular digital detoxes can refresh your perspective and recharge your energy, leaving you better equipped to tackle digital tasks with renewed vigour.

Incorporating Self-Care Practices

Digital Self-Care: Incorporating self-care practices into your digital routine is not just a luxury; it's a necessity for promoting digital well-being. Just as you schedule time for physical exercise and relaxation, plan regular intervals dedicated to digital self-care. This could include simple activities like organising your digital space. Declutter your desktop, sort through emails, and clean out unused apps. A tidy digital environment can reduce stress and improve efficiency.

Nurturing Mental Health: Engage in practices that calm your mind and reduce anxiety, such as mindfulness meditation apps or digital journals. These tools can provide guidance and structure, making it easier to manage stress and maintain emotional balance. Including moments of reflection in your daily routine allows you to process your thoughts and feelings, leading to a more harmonious relationship with technology.

Balancing Online and Offline Relationships

In-Person Connections: Don't forget the power of connecting with others in person. Despite the convenience and appeal of virtual communication, nothing beats face-to-face interactions for building solid relationships. Schedule regular meetups with friends and family to ensure your social life isn't entirely digital. Personal connections enrich your life in ways digital interactions can't fully replicate. Balancing online and offline relationships contributes to a more prosperous, more fulfilling existence.

Constructive Engagement with Online Communities

Kindness and Respect

Positive Interactions: Positive online community interactions can significantly enhance personal growth and success. Always remember to be kind and respectful. This might sound basic, but it's the foundation of any good interaction. Think before you type! If something isn't appropriate or considerate to say face-to-face, it probably isn't suitable for an online comment. By maintaining a respectful tone, you encourage others to do the same, creating a ripple effect of positivity. Just like a smile can be contagious in person, a kind word online can brighten someone's day and foster a welcoming community atmosphere.

Active Listening

Engaging Thoughtfully: Active listening is crucial. It may seem odd to talk about "listening" when most online interactions involve reading, but the principle remains the same. Take the time to understand the points others are making before jumping in with your own opinions. Acknowledge their perspectives, ask questions if something isn't clear, and contribute thoughtfully. This shows respect and genuine interest, which can lead to more meaningful conversations and stronger connections. Plus, you might learn something new and expand your horizons!

Offering Support and Encouragement

Building Community: Offer support and encouragement whenever possible. Online communities can often be places where individuals seek advice, share challenges, or celebrate successes. Celebrating others' achievements, offering a listening ear, or providing helpful feedback can make a big difference. Feeling supported and valued makes people more likely to remain active and engaged in the community. This sense of camaraderie not only benefits them but also helps in building a positive, nurturing environment for everyone involved.

Setting Boundaries

Protecting Mental Well-being: Navigating the digital world effectively also means setting boundaries. While engaging positively is essential, knowing when to step back is equally important. Not all online interactions will be pleasant, and there will be times when disengaging is the best course of action. If a conversation becomes toxic or you encounter persistent negativity, taking a break or walking away is okay. This protects your mental well-being and helps you stay focused on productive interactions without getting dragged down by negativity.

Joining Like-Minded Communities

Finding Your Tribe: Seek out communities that align with your values and interests. Joining groups or forums where members share similar passions or goals can lead to more positive experiences and fruitful interactions. You get to engage with content that matters to you and find peers who inspire and challenge you intellectually and creatively.

Fostering Inclusivity and Diversity

Encouraging Diverse Voices: Online spaces thrive harmoniously with different voices and perspectives. Actively welcoming new members, encouraging diverse opinions, and addressing exclusionary behaviour contribute to a richer, more vibrant community experience. Inclusiveness broadens the range of ideas and ensures everyone feels seen and heard, enhancing the quality of dialogue and learning for all participants.

Building Trust

Establishing Credibility: Building trust within online communities takes consistent effort. Trust is integral to any relationship, even in the digital realm. Being reliable, honest, and transparent in your communications helps establish this trust. Share information truthfully, keep commitments, and admit mistakes when they happen. These actions build credibility and create an environment where members feel safe to express themselves freely.

Understanding the Impact of Your Words

Practising Empathy: The anonymity of the internet can tempt people to act differently than they would in person. However, recognising that there's a natural person on the other side of the screen is crucial. Empathy goes a long way in preventing misunderstandings and conflicts. Always consider the potential effects of your comments, and strive to be constructive rather than critical.

Small Gestures of Positivity

Contributing to the Community: Positive online interactions can extend beyond verbal communication. Small gestures like sharing valuable resources, participating in community projects, or simply reacting positively to others' posts are not insignificant. They play a significant role in contributing to a positive atmosphere. These actions show that you value the community and are invested in its growth, encouraging others to do the same.

Continuous Self-Improvement

Reflect and Grow: Anyone seeking to foster positive interactions online should aim for continuous self-improvement. Reflecting on your digital behaviour, seeking feedback, and learning from past experiences are not just steps; they are a commitment to personal growth. They help you grow personally and improve your engagement skills. Like any other aspect of life, being proactive about self-improvement can lead to better relationships and tremendous success within the digital landscape.

By adopting these digital habits, individuals can harness the power of technology to support their personal growth and achieve tremendous success. So, we've talked about everything from taming the wild beast that is your social media feed to performing digital detoxes that would make even a monk proud. We've learned that mindful consumption of digital content isn't just about cutting down on cat videos (though cats can be very absorbing). It's about picking and choosing what fills your mind's buffet.

Your Digital Diet

Choosing Wisely: Remember when we suggested swapping out stressful accounts for those that inspire growth? Well, imagine your social media feeds as an all-you-can-eat salad bar. Yes, you heard me right — a salad bar. There's the not-so-healthy macaroni salad (negative news or toxic drama) and the fresh kale with avocado dressing (uplifting, educational content). Which one do you want more of in your life?

Real-World Repercussions

Understanding Digital Impact: As we sail forward, it's crucial to spotlight our position on this digital ship. We're fully anchored in believing that what you consume digitally has real-world repercussions. Unlike that five-layer chocolate cake, we know it's easy to downplay since digital calories are invisible — until they're not. Excessive screen time can turn into fatigue and burnout faster than you can say, "just one more episode."

Mental Well-being and Digital Consumption

Avoiding Echo Chambers: Spend too much time engulfed in an echo chamber, and you might start thinking the earth is flat, that pineapple belongs on pizza, or worse — that you'll never achieve anything because everyone else seems to have their lives perfectly Instagrammed.

Building a Better Community

Broadening Horizons: The stakes aren't just personal; they ripple outward. A community fed on diverse, thoughtful content is likely to be more empathetic, innovative, and resilient. On the other hand, echo chambers breed narrow-mindedness faster than bread left out in the rain grows Mold. So, step out of your comfort zone and look around. Read different viewpoints, engage with varied content, and keep your mental horizons broad.

Training for Success

Digital Olympics: Finally, here's a little nugget to chew on. What if we started treating our digital habits like training for the Olympics? Okay, maybe not the Olympics unless there's suddenly a category for thumb war scrolling. But think about it — mindful consumption could be our superpower. By curating our digital space thoughtfully, setting boundaries like a pro, and taking purposeful breaks, we create a path towards success paved with golden pixels.

Taking the First Step

Starting Today: As you ponder these thoughts, consider what's stopping you from making these changes. The journey to better digital habits starts with a single click or a power-off button.

Final Thoughts

In this book, we've explored essential strategies to help you thrive in your first job. By adapting to workplace culture, building professional relationships, managing your Time effectively, and setting clear career goals, you're well on your way to success. Understanding and respecting your organisation's values, norms, and expectations will help you integrate smoothly and build strong connections with colleagues. These efforts pave the way for personal growth and contribute significantly to your overall job satisfaction and career progression.

Embracing Workplace Culture

Adapting to the culture of your workplace is foundational to your success. Each organisation has unique values and norms that guide behaviour and decision-making. By embracing these principles, you align yourself with the company's mission and become a valued team member. As you integrate into the workplace, observe and adapt to explicit and implicit rules. This approach helps you fit in and fosters a sense of belonging and mutual respect with your colleagues.

Building Professional Relationships

Building and nurturing professional relationships is crucial. Networking, seeking mentorship, and effective communication can accelerate your career progression and open doors to new opportunities. Engage actively in networking events, seek guidance from experienced professionals, and maintain consistent, meaningful interactions with your peers. These connections provide support, offer valuable insights, and can significantly enhance your professional growth.

Mastering Time Management

Effective time management is another key to thriving in your first job. Prioritising tasks, overcoming procrastination, and setting specific deadlines can help you stay organised and productive. Use tools like the Eisenhower Matrix to categorise tasks and focus on what truly matters. Implement strategies to limit distractions and take regular breaks to maintain productivity and well-being. By mastering time management, you can handle your responsibilities efficiently and reduce stress.

Setting and Achieving Career Goals

Setting clear, actionable career goals provides direction and motivation. Define what you want to achieve in the short and long term, and plan to reach these milestones. Seek feedback from mentors and supervisors to refine your goals and ensure they remain relevant. Celebrate your achievements, learn from setbacks, and stay committed to continuous improvement. Setting stretch goals and regularly reviewing your objectives will keep you aligned with your aspirations and responsive to changing circumstances.

Continuous Learning and Adaptation

Remember, excelling in your first job is a journey that requires continuous learning and adaptation. Stay curious and open to new experiences. Seek feedback and use it constructively to grow. Embrace opportunities for professional development, whether through formal training, new projects, or learning from your peers. Your willingness to adapt and learn will help you overcome challenges and position you for long-term success in your career.

Building a Solid Foundation

The strategies discussed in this book are designed to help you navigate the complexities of your first job and build a strong foundation for your career. By adapting to workplace culture, fostering professional relationships, managing your Time effectively, and setting clear goals, you equip yourself with the tools needed to succeed. The foundation you build now will serve as a solid base for a rewarding and fulfilling career.

Conclusion

As you embark on your professional journey, remember that success is not a destination but a continuous process of growth and adaptation. Implement the strategies discussed in this book, stay committed to your goals, and remain open to learning and development. By doing so, you will not only thrive in your first job but also pave the way for a successful and fulfilling career. The efforts you invest in today will yield significant rewards in the future, ensuring that you achieve your professional aspirations and find fulfilment in your chosen field.

The Journey Begins with You

As you reach the end of "Life-Changing Lessons I Learned Too Late: Wisdom, I Wish I Knew at My First Job," remember that this is not just a book but a call to action. Your career, life, and dreams are all within your reach. Every chapter and lesson shared here is meant to equip you with the tools and insights to fast-forward your professional journey and enrich your personal life.

Embrace Your Power

Imagine the power you hold in your hands right now. You've learned about adapting to workplace culture, building professional relationships, managing time effectively, and more. These aren't just lessons; they are your secret weapons. You have the potential to transform your career and your life with the wisdom you now possess. It's your turn to embrace these lessons and let them guide you toward the success and fulfilment you deserve.

"The best time to plant a tree was 20 years ago. The second best time is now." — Chinese Proverb

Apply What You've Learned

Reflect on what resonated with you the most. Was it important to set clear goals or perhaps the value of patience and self-compassion? Take those insights and make them actionable. Start setting those goals, practising gratitude, and living authentically. Your professional journey is a canvas, and you are the artist. Paint it with the colours of your dreams, aspirations, and newfound wisdom.

Example: If you learned the value of time management, begin by organising your daily tasks. Create a schedule that prioritises your most important activities and stick to it. Celebrate each completed task, no matter how small, and watch your productivity soar.

Believe in Your Potential

One of the most significant lessons in this book is believing in yourself. Your potential is limitless. The only barriers are the ones you set for yourself. Break free from limiting beliefs and replace them with empowering thoughts. You are capable of achieving greatness. Every step you take towards self-improvement and professional growth is a testament to your dedication and resilience.

Start each day with affirmations reinforcing your belief in your abilities. Say, "I am capable of achieving my goals," and "I embrace every opportunity for growth."

Build Your Support Network

Remember, you are not alone on this journey. Surround yourself with people who believe in you and your vision. Seek mentorship, build strong professional relationships, and engage with a community that supports your growth. Together, you can achieve more than you ever imagined.

"If you want to go fast, go alone. If you want to go far, go together." — African Proverb

Celebrate Your Progress

Take time to celebrate your victories, both big and small. Every milestone reached, and every challenge overcome deserves recognition. Celebrating your progress keeps you motivated and reminds you of how far you've come. It's a powerful way to boost your morale and continue striving for excellence.

Example: Did you successfully manage a challenging project? Treat yourself to something special. Maybe it's a favourite meal, a relaxing day off, or simply reflecting on your achievement.

Continue the Journey

The end of this book is the beginning of a new chapter in your life. Continue to learn, grow, and evolve. Embrace continuous learning, show initiative, and maintain a positive attitude. Your career is a journey; every day is an opportunity to move closer to your goals.

Live Your Best Life

Ultimately, this book is about living your best life. Embrace the abundance of who you are, unleash your inner dancer, and take nothing for granted. Life is precious, and every moment is an opportunity to grow, love, and achieve. Your dreams are within your grasp. Go out there and make them a reality.

Take a moment now to write down three actions you will take this week to apply what you've learned. Commit to these actions and watch as your life begins to transform.

Thank You for Taking This Journey

Thank you for embarking on this journey with me. Your commitment to self-improvement and professional growth is inspiring. Remember, you are the author of your own story. Write it with passion, purpose, and the wisdom you now hold.

"The future belongs to those who believe in the beauty of their dreams." — Eleanor Roosevelt

Your Vision Awaits

Your vision is waiting for you. Are you ready to make it a reality? You are unstoppable with the lessons you've learned, the goals you've set, and the belief in your potential. Go forth and create the life and career you've always dreamed of. Your journey to success begins now.

Take the first step today. Embrace your vision, believe in yourself, and start living the life you were meant to lead. Your potential is limitless, and your future is bright.

Conclusion

As you close this book, remember that it's the start of a new beginning. Armed with wisdom and driven by a compelling vision, you have everything you need to fast forward your career and achieve your dreams. Embrace the journey, celebrate your progress, and always strive to be the best version of yourself. Your success story is waiting to be written — go out there and write it!

Example from the Life of Steve Jobs

Steve Jobs, the visionary co-founder of Apple Inc., exemplifies the power of a compelling vision in the business world. Jobs envisioned creating revolutionary technology that would change how people live and work. This vision drove him to push boundaries and innovate relentlessly.

Envision Your Ideal Future: Visualize Your Dreams in Vivid Detail

Jobs imagined a future where technology was intuitive, beautiful, and seamlessly integrated into everyday life. He visualised products that were functional, aesthetically pleasing, and easy to use. This vision was the driving force behind iconic products like the iPhone, iPad, and Mac.

"The people who are crazy enough to think they can change the world are the ones who do." — Steve Jobs

Set Clear, Specific Goals

Jobs set clear and specific goals to realise his vision. He wanted Apple to create groundbreaking products that would lead the industry and set new standards for innovation. Instead of a vague goal like "create great products," Jobs aimed to "revolutionise personal computing" and "create the best user experience."

Example: Instead of a vague goal like "make a better phone," Jobs set a specific goal to create the iPhone, which combined a phone, an iPod, and an internet communicator into one device.

Break Down Your Big Dreams: Create Sub-Goals

Jobs understood that achieving his grand vision required breaking it down into manageable steps. This meant setting sub-goals like developing a touchscreen interface, integrating powerful software, and designing an elegant hardware form for the iPhone.

"The journey of a thousand miles begins with one step." — Lao Tzu

Celebrate Small Wins

Jobs celebrated every milestone that brought Apple closer to its vision. From the successful launch of the Macintosh in 1984 to the introduction of the iPod in 2001, each success was a step towards realising his larger goals. Celebrating these achievements kept the team motivated and focused.

Example: When the iPhone was successfully demonstrated for the first time, Jobs celebrated this milestone, knowing it was a crucial step towards revolutionising the mobile phone industry.

Examine and Empower Your Beliefs

Identify Limiting Beliefs

Jobs identified and overcame limiting beliefs throughout his career. He refused to accept "good enough" and pushed for excellence, believing that Apple could create products that would change the world.

"Whether you think you can, or you think you can't— you're right." — Henry Ford

Use Affirmations to Shift Your Mindset

Jobs constantly reaffirmed his belief in Apple's ability to innovate and lead. His famous "Think Different" mantra encapsulated this mindset, encouraging himself and his team to break free from conventional thinking.

Example: Jobs often repeated, "Stay hungry, stay foolish," to inspire a mindset of curiosity and boldness in pursuit of their vision.

Surround Yourself with Supportive People

Build a Positive Network

Jobs surrounded himself with a talented and dedicated team at Apple. He built a culture of innovation and excellence by hiring individuals who shared his passion and vision. This network of supportive people was crucial in bringing his ideas to life.

"Surround yourself with only people who are going to lift you higher." — Oprah Winfrey

Share Your Vision

Jobs shared his vision widely, both within Apple and with the public. He inspired his team and attracted loyal customers and supporters by articulating his dreams. His keynote presentations were legendary for their ability to communicate his vision and generate excitement.

Example: Jobs' presentations, such as the unveiling of the iPhone in 2007, effectively communicated his vision and inspired millions worldwide.

Implementing These Principles

Daily Visualization

Jobs practised visualisation by constantly imagining the future he wanted to create. This practice kept his vision vivid and motivated him to take action every day.

Consistent Goal Setting and Reviewing

Jobs regularly reviewed and adjusted his goals, ensuring they aligned with his vision. This consistent focus helped Apple stay on track and adapt to new opportunities and challenges.

Affirmations and Positive Self-Talk

Jobs used affirmations and positive self-talk to maintain his confidence and focus. His belief in his vision and his team's abilities drove them to achieve extraordinary results.

Engage with Your Support Network

Jobs stayed actively engaged with his support network, seeking advice, feedback, and inspiration from mentors, colleagues, and industry leaders. This engagement helped him navigate challenges and stay motivated.

Conclusion

Steve Jobs' life is a testament to the power of a compelling vision combined with determination and strategic action. By envisioning his ideal future, setting clear and specific goals, breaking them down into manageable steps, empowering his beliefs, and surrounding himself with supportive people, Jobs transformed the technology industry and left an enduring legacy. Embrace these principles, and you, too, can unleash your potential and create the life of your dreams. Your vision is waiting—are you ready to make it a reality?

Example from the Life of Dhirubhai Ambani

Dhirubhai Ambani, the founder of Reliance Industries, is a stellar example of how building strong professional relationships can unlock immense opportunities. Ambani built one of India's largest conglomerates from humble beginnings, largely through his ability to connect with people and forge strategic partnerships.

Ambani's journey began in Yemen, where he worked as a clerk. During his time there, he cultivated relationships with local traders and businessmen, gaining insights into the trade and commerce industry. These connections were instrumental when he returned to India and started his own business.

One of Ambani's significant achievements was building a robust support system of stakeholders, including suppliers, investors, and employees. His charismatic personality and genuine interest in others helped him gain the trust and support of those around him. Ambani believed in nurturing relationships with everyone, from high-ranking officials to ordinary employees, understanding that each connection could be crucial to his business's success.

A notable example of Ambani's relationship-building skills was his interaction with the Indian government and bureaucracy. He adeptly navigated the complex regulatory environment by forming strong ties with policymakers and leveraging these relationships to gain favourable terms for his business ventures. This strategic networking enabled

Reliance to expand rapidly and become a dominant player in various industries.

Ambani also valued mentorship and learning from others. He sought guidance from experienced businessmen and industry leaders, using their insights to make informed decisions and avoid common pitfalls. His ability to seek and act on advice from his mentors contributed significantly to his business acumen and strategic thinking.

"Growth has no limit at Reliance. I keep revising my vision. Only when you dream it, you can do it." — Dhirubhai Ambani

Dhirubhai Ambani's dedication to helping others was another key aspect of his success. He believed in adding value to others through business deals, mentorship, or community initiatives. This approach strengthened his professional relationships and built a positive reputation for Reliance Industries as a company that cared about its stakeholders.

Conclusion

Building strong professional relationships is essential for unlocking opportunities and creating a robust support system. You can cultivate meaningful relationships that will benefit your career by being genuine, offering value, and actively participating in networking activities. As John C. Maxwell aptly stated, "People may hear your words, but they feel your attitude." Approach relationship-building with a positive attitude and genuine intent, and you will see wide doors of opportunity open. Dhirubhai Ambani's success story is a testament to the power of strong relationships in achieving business success. Embrace these principles, and watch your professional network and opportunities grow.

Example from the Life of a Sports Icon:

Virat Kohli

Virat Kohli, one of the most successful cricketers of all time, exemplifies the principle that "health is wealth." His dedication to physical and mental well-being has been a cornerstone of his extraordinary career.

When Kohli began his career, he was talented but lacked the physical fitness required to consistently compete at the highest level. Realising this, he transformed his lifestyle by prioritising his health. Kohli adopted a rigorous fitness regime with strength training, cardio, and flexibility exercises. This commitment to regular exercise significantly improved his endurance, strength, and overall performance on the field.

Kohli's diet also plays a crucial role in his fitness. He follows a balanced diet of lean proteins, vegetables, and healthy fats while avoiding junk food and sugary drinks. His disciplined approach to nutrition has helped him maintain peak physical condition and recover quickly from injuries.

"I understood that health is the most important thing in life, and without it, you cannot achieve anything." — Virat Kohli

Kohli values mental health equally. He practices mindfulness and meditation to manage stress and maintain emotional balance. These practices help him stay focused, calm, and composed, especially under the immense pressure of international cricket.

Kohli also emphasises the importance of adequate sleep and hydration. He ensures he gets enough rest to recover from the game's physical demands and stays hydrated to keep his body functioning optimally.

Through his journey, Kohli has demonstrated that prioritising health leads to increased productivity, a better quality of life, and emotional stability. His success on the cricket field is a testament to the fact that physical and mental well-being are fundamental to achieving one's goals and living a fulfilling life.

Conclusion

Prioritising physical and mental health through regular exercise, a balanced diet, and stress management is essential for a fulfilling and productive life. Strategies to enhance well-being include:

- Regular exercise

- Balanced diet

- Stress management

Incorporating these into your daily routine can improve your well-being, reduce healthcare costs, and enjoy a higher quality of life. As Ralph Waldo Emerson wisely said, "The first wealth is health." Make health a priority, and you'll reap the benefits of a rich and satisfying life. Virat Kohli's story is a powerful example of how focusing on health can lead to extraordinary achievements and a fulfilling life.

Life-Changing Lessons I Learned Too Late:
Wisdom, I wish I had Known At My First Job

Example from the Life of Ratan Tata

Ratan Tata, the former chairman of Tata Sons, is a shining example of how practising gratitude can lead to happiness and resilience. Throughout his illustrious career, Tata has exemplified humility, generosity, and gratitude, which have been pivotal to his success and legacy.

Ratan Tata's journey began with his education at Cornell University and Harvard Business School. Upon his return to India, he joined the Tata Group, where he worked his way up through various roles. Despite his privileged background, Tata has always felt grateful for the opportunities and support he received.

Tata's approach to leadership is deeply rooted in gratitude. He consistently acknowledges the contributions of his employees, often attributing the success of the Tata Group to their hard work and dedication. This appreciation has fostered strong loyalty and motivation within the organisation.

"I don't believe in making the right decisions. I take decisions and then make them right." — Ratan Tata

One notable example of Tata's gratitude in action is his response to the 26/11 Mumbai terrorist attacks. The Taj Mahal Palace Hotel, a part of the Tata Group, was one of the attack targets. In the aftermath, Tata personally visited the families of all affected employees, offering support and ensuring they received full medical and financial assistance. This compassionate response demonstrated his deep gratitude and care for his employees, reinforcing their trust and loyalty.

Tata's philanthropic efforts further illustrate his gratitude. He has been instrumental in driving the Tata Group's commitment to corporate social responsibility, ensuring that a significant portion of the company's profits is dedicated to social causes. Through initiatives in education, healthcare, and rural development, Tata has shown his gratitude by giving back to society and improving the lives of countless individuals.

In his personal life, Ratan Tata practices gratitude through mindfulness and reflection. He often speaks about the importance of staying grounded and appreciating the simple joys of life. This mindset has helped him navigate the challenges and pressures of leading a global conglomerate with grace and resilience.

Conclusion

Practising gratitude regularly leads to greater happiness and resilience. Key ways to cultivate a grateful mindset include:

- Keep a gratitude journal

- Express gratitude to others

- Practise mindfulness

- Reflect on positive experiences

- Create a gratitude ritual

- Use visual reminders

- Volunteer

- Focus on the positive

- Celebrate small wins

- Practise self-compassion

As the Roman philosopher Cicero said, "Gratitude is not only the greatest of virtues but the parent of all others." Embrace gratitude, and you will unlock a richer, more fulfilling life filled with happiness and resilience. Ratan Tata's life exemplifies how practising gratitude can lead to extraordinary achievements and a legacy of positive impact.

Example from the Life of a Great Scientist:

Vikram Sarabhai

Vikram Sarabhai, the father of the Indian space program, is an inspiring example of pursuing one's passion to lead a satisfying and rewarding life. Sarabhai's passion for science and technology drove him to establish India's space research initiatives and achieve remarkable milestones.

Early Life and Passion for Science

Vikram Sarabhai was born in 1919 in Ahmedabad, India. From a young age, he showed a keen interest in science and innovation. He pursued his education in Physics at the University of Cambridge, where he was exposed to cutting-edge research and technology. This experience further fuelled his passion for scientific exploration.

Pursuing His Passion for Space Science

After returning to India, Sarabhai identified the potential of space technology to address the country's developmental challenges. He was determined to establish a space program to benefit India and contribute to global scientific advancements. His passion for space science became the driving force behind the founding of the Indian Space Research Organisation (ISRO) in 1969.

Notable Achievements of Vikram Sarabhai

1. **Founding ISRO**: Vikram Sarabhai is best known for founding the Indian Space Research Organisation

(ISRO) in 1969. His vision was to harness space technology for national development, making India a global player in space research.

2. **Establishing the Physical Research Laboratory (PRL)**: In 1947, Sarabhai established the Physical Research Laboratory in Ahmedabad, which became a premier institution for space science and technology research.

3. **Initiating the Indian Satellite Program**: Under Sarabhai's leadership, India launched its first satellite, Aryabhata, in 1975. Although launched after his death, this milestone directly resulted from his groundwork and vision.

4. **Setting Up the Thumba Equatorial Rocket Launching Station (TERLS)**: In 1963, Sarabhai set up TERLS near Thiruvananthapuram, which became the first rocket launching station in India. This facility was crucial for India's space missions and research.

5. **Promoting Satellite Television for Education**: Sarabhai pioneered using satellite television for educational purposes. The Satellite Instructional Television Experiment (SITE) in 1975-76, which used NASA's ATS-6 satellite, was one of the largest sociological experiments, reaching millions of Indian villagers.

6. **Advancing India's Nuclear Power**: Sarabhai also played a significant role in India's nuclear power

development. He succeeded Homi Bhabha as the chairman of the Atomic Energy Commission of India and focused on peaceful nuclear energy applications.

7. **Establishing the Indian Institute of Management (IIM), Ahmedabad**: Sarabhai was instrumental in setting up the IIM in Ahmedabad in 1961. This institution has become one of the leading business schools in India and globally.

8. **Promoting Space Research through International Collaboration**: Sarabhai's efforts led to significant international collaborations, including partnerships with NASA and other global space agencies, which were crucial for India's space program's growth.

9. **Awards and Recognitions**: Sarabhai received several prestigious awards, including the Padma Bhushan in 1966 and the Padma Vibhushan (posthumously) in 1972, recognising his immense contributions to science and technology.

Conclusion

Vikram Sarabhai's achievements laid the foundation for India's space and nuclear programs. His visionary leadership and dedication to science and technology continue to inspire future generations of scientists and engineers. Through his notable achievements, Sarabhai exemplified the profound impact of pursuing one's passion and the far-reaching benefits it can bring to society and the nation.

About the Author

Ignatious Antony, a visionary technocrat, has embarked on an extraordinary journey of engineering brilliance! His career, deeply rooted in the prestigious Indian Space Research Organisation, saw him excel as the Deputy Director at the Vikram Sarabhai Space Centre (VSSC) in Thiruvananthapuram, Kerala. Post-retirement, his professional adventure continued as the Vice President (Technical) at a renowned Electronics System R&D organisation, where he's been passionately mentoring a dynamic team of professionals, young engineers, and highly talented technocrats for the past decade.

As a highly esteemed Professional Engineer, Ignatious has led significant teams, pioneering the development and certification of avionics systems for ISRO's ambitious rocket launches. His invaluable contributions in developing mission computers, GNC systems, and other avionics systems for ISRO's launch vehicles are legendary. He also served as the Chief of the Quality Assurance Entity at Vikram Sarabhai Space Centre, ISRO, showcasing his unwavering commitment to excellence.

His life, both personal and professional, is a tapestry woven with threads of remarkable encounters—close interactions with successful professionals, engineers, rocket scientists, business executives, leaders, and senior administrative personnel, alongside highly skilled launch vehicle technicians. As a space scientist, Ignatious has gained firsthand insights into the lives of highly talented and successful individuals and those whose stars have not shone as brightly.

These diverse interactions ignited a profound curiosity within him, driving Ignatious to unravel the enigma of success. His philosophy, "Excellence is everywhere. You see only what you look for. Especially search inside; you can see surprising wonders," perfectly encapsulates his approach to life and work.

Ignatious is also a prolific writer who has presented numerous technical papers at national and international conferences. His extensive travels, both within the country and abroad, have further enriched his perspectives.

Ignatious Antony resides with his loving wife in the serene city of Thiruvananthapuram, Kerala. Together, they cherish their two children's joy and their three grandchildren's boundless energy.

PS: Email-Id of the author: ignatious.luck@gmail.com